W9-BAS-538

MUSIC IN WORSHIP

The Use of Music in the Church Service

by

JOSEPH N. ASHTON

Formerly Associate Professor of Musical History and Theory in Brown University; also Lecturer in Music at Wellesley College.

THE PILGRIM PRESS

BOSTON   CHICAGO

CONTENTS

PART ONE

PART TWO

PREFACE

THIS BOOK had its origin in a course on the history, theory, and practice of church music which I conducted at Brown University during the period of my service on its faculty.

The present volume is devoted to consideration of the principles and practice of church music. In it I have aimed to set forth the essential function of church music and to present certain means of attaining it. In general, Part One has to do with the principles of church music, Part Two with the application of these.

As the musical conditions of the practice of church music are so diverse and the methods of its use so varied, it has been found desirable to select a definite type of service for exemplification. For this purpose the order of worship commonly used in the regular Sunday morning service of a fairly large non-ritualistic church has been chosen inasmuch as it provides the freest and widest scope and offers the greatest opportunity for constructive suggestion.

J. N. A.

Andover, Massachusetts

CHAPTER I

CHURCH MUSIC

MUSIC is more extensively employed in the church service today than ever before. Approximately one third of the period consists of musical items. In liturgical churches there has been a general tendency in recent times to employ more music and to use it more expressively, while in non-liturgical churches sections of the service have been developed in which music is increasingly used. This larger use of music in public worship calls for the expenditure of much effort and money. Given larger scope in the church service, music is more and more coming to be regarded as an essential for which regular appropriations are made. Despite all this, the results are not satisfactory. Church music is far from being what it might and should be.

CONCEPTIONS of church music and attitudes toward it vary widely and in many ways. As a consequence great differences are to be found in its practice. An enumeration of these discloses various aspects and phases, some of which are of great import while others are only superficial.

Not uncommonly church music is regarded merely as a matter of traditional routine. The musical parts of the service are treated with a sort of deferential tolerance—unless they become unendurable musically. Church music is accounted a conventional interpolation, something considered necessary in a certain sequence and proportion in each service. This conception derives either from long tradition the roots of which are dead, or from recent custom which has come from innovations made from time to time, more or less casually, without thought of a sound and consistent practice. This view of church

1

music treats it as something without significance—harmless to be sure, yet somehow indispensable.

Others look upon church music as padding to fill up time in what is designated as "the opening exercises." For such, the first part of the service—the part in which music has its chief place—is a preliminary section, not one in which music is employed directly and profoundly for religious purpose. Rather, it is used to effect a general emotional warming up. Not infrequently congregational and choir music is introduced in the service and placed in alteration with clerical parts in order to give diversity to the proceedings and offset a tediousness which the exercises might otherwise have. For such as hold this view church music, especially choir music, is likely to be, as Lowell Mason once put it, "a kind of interlude in religious worship."

Then there is the *laissez-faire* treatment. Church music is taken to be a trifling matter, or it may be a thorny matter in which it is wise not to become entangled. In either case there is no clear and generally recognized ideal as to its proper function. Hopelessly confused and endlessly perplexing, church music is felt to be not susceptible to or perhaps worthy of serious concern, and is given over to those who are willing to engage in it. Instead of being purposefully and intelligently directed by the church as a corporate religious body, music is left to drift and shift for itself.

In contrast to those who hold church music in low esteem and treat it with indifference, there are others who cultivate it zealously, enthusiastically, and even at times extravagantly. By many it is considered chiefly as an attraction, popular musical appeal being largely the criterion. It is, in fact, treated as belonging rather more to the field of church advertising than strictly to that of religious worship. To attract attendance, special musical programs are arranged, more or less popular and sometimes even of semi-secular character, intended to "brighten" the services and to please the assembled auditors. Such music is likely to have little religious relevancy and to give to the church the character of a place of entertainment or a concert hall. Some of those employing church music as an attraction rather than as a means of worship use it as a decoy to gather an audience, hoping that through the preaching that follows a distinctly religious appeal may be made to those who have been drawn to the church service by the prospect of pleasant music. There are even those who rest content if only they can succeed in drawing a large attendance to hear vocal and instrumental music.

Then again, church music is often treated chiefly with reference to the participants. It is regarded as a vehicle for individual display or group exhibition. Individuals or groups are welcomed by the church to "furnish music" for the service. The service, in fact, is used as an opportunity to afford regular or occasional hearings for soloists and quartets or for choral groups, adult and juvenile. In the one case, the music of the church often takes on the character of salon music and that of the concert hall, while in the other, there is unfortunately very likely to be greater interest in maintaining an activity within the church than in making it actually minister to the worship of the congregation. The congregation may be willing to permit those who wish to sing in the service to do so for their own gratification—and such singing may also be for the pleasure of the congregation—but neither of these purposes is that for which music has been admitted into the sanctuary. By giving such lower considerations too much weight, the fundamental function of church music is lost. It should not be overlooked, moreover, that such a use of music may become a real encumbrance or a positive detriment in the service, for it may not prove satisfactory even from the musical standpoint.

Related to this view of church music is that which commits it to the management of some of the more well-to-do members of the congregation who are willing to contribute to its financial support, the church thus allowing its music and those parts of its services in which music enters to be made a matter of patronage. Often highly priced soloists or a quartet are secured,

3

a recital organist is engaged, or a special choral organization is set up. These artists become centres of attraction and church music develops into a luxury enjoyed by the congregation through the generosity of those who maintain it as a hobby. Such church music is likely either to be over-refined, or else to become flamboyant in fussed-up ostentation. In neither case is it a source of power for animating worship.

Church music is, furthermore, sometimes conceived as being a gentle, refined art, permitted "for the comforting of such that delight in music," or to quote the quaint title of the Psalmody collection of George Thomas Smart, about 1795, organist of St. James Chapel, London—"A Divine Amusement." Surely, in these days, church music should be something more than an innocent, harmless, and pleasant pastime, simply sweet.

By some the aesthetic and cultural aspects of church music are strongly stressed and are often apparently regarded as well-nigh basic. Now the aesthetic and the cultural elements are in some ways related to religion; but they are by no means identical with it. Definitions of beauty, culture, and religion vary. While it is not our intention to discuss such matters here, we do wish to assert that the value of church music does not depend fundamentally upon the aesthetic gratification it affords, and also that it does not essentially justify itself by being regarded as a means of elevating the musical taste of the congregation and community. Both of these ends may be secured entirely apart from church activity or religious interest. Musical education and advancement are indeed highly desirable; they are valuable to the community, and also to the church in its efforts to secure more effective church music. Though they should not be ignored or lightly considered, they are nevertheless not of prime concern for the church.

Another conception of church music is that which treats it as a matter of decoration, a sacrifice, or an offering to God. This view is not without propriety and value. The temples of the gods are always made beautiful, and man in approaching the Highest apparels himself in becoming attire. But the outward aspect of things may be unduly emphasized; our church music may become something wholly objective in character. Though it is indeed right that we make our services as worthy as possible of Him to whom they are offered, though we may be sure that He is well-pleased to have us seek to dwell consciously in His special Presence in a manner which sensibly accords with His nature, nevertheless, we cannot think of God as being gratified with our music as such. Music is rather a medium of expression and communion. In this respect it should be worthy—a consideration ever to be kept to the fore. Church music as offering will, by virtue of the character of their worship and their conception of the church, be more distinctly appropriate for some religious bodies than for others. This subject will be fully considered later. Though valid to a certain extent and in a certain way, the conception of church music as decoration, offering or sacrifice is, nevertheless, incomplete and imperfect.

Differences of conception regarding church music are not confined to the laity, the clergy, and the rank and file of church musicians; they are to be found among eminent professional church musicians and composers of distinguished achievement. Some of these have even denied that there really can be any such thing as church music! Yet these selfsame persons have still continued to conduct, to compose, and to discuss church music with apparent sincerity! Their difficulty, we may say parenthetically, is largely a matter of definition: they are dissatisfied with objective material labels—and they are right.

Such are some of the views which we find more or less consciously held; such are some of the conceptions upon which our practice of church music is built. Can there, amid such diversities of opinion, be any fundamental principles or anything like a clear-cut ideal of church music? We believe that there can be; but in the search to determine such principles and ideals regard must be given to their essential character. Church music is many-sided. It is essentially a compound problem, a problem at once in the field of religion and in the field of music. Many of the views which have just been set forth represent vital phases. Some of these accentuate factors which are more or less primary; others are concerned with those which are distinctly secondary or merely incidental. They are not all on the same plane. In seeking an ideal and formulating principles of church music we ought to appraise at their respective values the conceptions which have elements of inherent vitality. An ideal of church music, as in other fields, must be concerned with the qualities peculiar to it. Since church music is in its very nature extremely subjective, and for its very existence has ever to be recreated, the ideal will naturally be less concrete than in many other areas of human thought and activity.

THE IDEAL of church music is found in its function. This function is religious: to bring to stronger and clearer consciousness and to greater vitality our inherent religious nature. At the heart of church music must be the consciousness of this religious nature: the sense of the divine, of goodness and righteousness, of the Almighty, the Eternal; the sense of exaltation of human life to the divine, and accompanying this the feeling of humility into which such a sense must lead us. There is in all true church music a spirit of adoration, aspiration and reverence, and a sense of assurance. To aid the soul to become more keenly and deeply conscious of itself, its supreme personal quality, its high and enduring worth, is the ideal of church music. This is its mission. It is for this purpose that music has been admitted to the sanctuary. In seeking to attain its function in the service of religion, music is an agent both for expression and for impression.

Such is the ideal of church music. But in the nature of things this ideal will be variously realized, for since the church includes "all sorts and conditions of men," there will be great dissimilarities in human background and human outlook, wide variations in religious thought, tradition, and training, and also large differences in musical facilities, responsiveness, and appreciation. There are within the church, moreover, different church-music traditions, different practices and procedures

6

which are pertinent to this and that religious group. When, for instance, we compare as possible extremes the work and methods of the Salvation Army with that of a Cathedral Church and consider the music appropriate to each group, it is obvious that there cannot be a single, universal standard equally appropriate to all, but that there will properly be various standards and types of church music.

As both religion and music are such intimate experiences, deeply personal and subjective, we are naturally prone to identify ideal with standard or type in church music. We tend to take it for granted that that which inspires, moves and uplifts us must of necessity act in the same or at least in a similar way with others. But obviously such is not the fact. It is inevitable, therefore, that while there may be one ideal for church music there will be a variety of standards and types. The ideal will be realized variously and will be of varied quality.

Standards and types of church music are, so to speak, crystallizations of the ideal out of this or that solution. They have to do with actual practice under given conditions. More definite and concrete than ideals, standards need not, on that account, be mechanical or merely formal, any more than ideals, on account of their nature, need be visionary and unreal. The ideal finds its realization in the type. This means that there will be a number of types or standards, and not a single, universal standard. Failure to realize this basic fact makes futile any attempt at a systematic and comprehensive consideration of church music.

Always, and in every instance there must be sincerity as the basis of every true use of church music. This is the touchstone. Sincerity, utter sincerity, is an essential feature in religion, and it should be taken as the indispensable criterion in the field of church music. Situations will vary religiously and musically, as will also the precise manner and means of realizing the ideal; but whatever the situation, the practice of genuine church music should be such as to ring true to its high function and such as to attain its essential purpose.

CHAPTER II

FOUR FACTORS IN CHURCH MUSIC

FOUR FACTORS enter into church music: the musical, the conceptual, the ceremonial, and the associational. The precise character and quality of each of these will vary in different instances; they will be present in different proportions, but in one form or another they are everywhere to be found.

It is not by mere accident that music has always been used in religious worship, for religion and music arise from the same general part of our being. Religion is the most intimate of all human experiences, and music is the most intimate of the arts. Music is at once the most subjective, and the least concrete of all the arts; its subjectiveness is the most personal, its substance the least tangible. It has the very valuable property of stimulating the emotions and strengthening consciousness, yet at the same time regulating them through the sense of balance and proportion inherent in the art of music itself. Music is thus the ideal art for religious worship.

There is always a tendency to regard the musical composition itself as the essential and sole concern in church music. To some, the whole problem appears to be that of determining what music to use. It is because of this undue estimation of the musical composition in church music that some composers of church music have come to declare that there is no such thing as church music. Now, no music is in the strictest sense of the word religious. In fact, no thing, no act even, is religious in itself. Religion inheres only in the human spirit. But music and action in so far as they are the expressions and embodiments of the religious spirit may on that account be so closely related to the religious as to take on a religious aspect. So it is that while, on the one hand, the identity of religion with

8

music is not to be affirmed, yet on the other hand, the close relationship leading to the embodiment and functioning of religion through art is not to be denied.

While it is not possible to designate a given composition or a given type of music as absolutely and inevitably religious, it it possible to make some generalizations. Speaking broadly, religion as we find it in worship has a distinctive mood. It is reflective, aspirational, devout, earnest, dignified, noble. The mood which is characteristic of worship may find its counterpart in the realm of music—music which is meditative, tender, elevated, controlled, dignified, resolute—a counterpart which gives glow and fervor and also additional expressiveness to the religious. Only in so far as music or anything else may become a medium or means of conveying or embodying the religious spirit and religious experience may it be truly termed "religious." It is most desirable that it be as pertinent as possible to this purpose. The musical should be a vital element in church music. But it is not the only one.

ANOTHER FACTOR in church music is the conceptual. To designate this, take for example, the religious acts of adoration, aspiration, supplication, and dedication. In adoration there must be that which is adored, in aspiration that which is aspired to, and in supplication and dedication that which is earnestly desired or is resolved upon. Now it is this which is adored or aspired to, or is sought in supplication, or to which we dedicate ourselves, that constitutes the essential conceptual basis of worship necessary in church music. It is this, which is spiritually objective in one's religious consciousness, and not merely that which is purely mental, that the word "conceptual" is used here to designate. The conceptual factor, it is to be noted, may be couched in poetical, dramatic, symbolic or dogmatic expression, or it may be present indirectly through associational recall or otherwise. Such a religious factor is requisite to give the music of the church a quality and character which differentiates it from music in general and constitutes it specifically church music.

9

MUSIC IN WORSHIP

A THIRD FACTOR in church music is the ceremonial. This element is derived and takes its character from that reverent attitude and mood which is inherent in worship. The very nature of religious worship differentiates it from other activities. The sense of reverence, sublimity, awe, and worth, the feeling of tenderness, of humility and exaltation, the activity of conscious aspiration which is present in worship, raises it to a plane above ordinary living. This emotional attitude and mood which give an increased reality-feeling to religion and worship are what we wish to designate by the word ceremonial. Such ceremonial sense is normal in religious worship. Other ceremonial there is—physical movements and postures, interpretative and symbolic action intended to serve as "an outward expression of an inward grace," often elaborated into an extensive system. This sort of ceremonial, which the word generally suggests, is relatively objective; in so far as it is removed from the subjective sense in which we wish to use the word, it becomes mechanical and has dangers. Ceremonial, as the word is here used, is not this more or less outward means of expression of religious worship, but an inherent and accompanying part of worship itself, sustaining a necessary and vital relation to it. It is an encompassing sense. It is, so to speak, the sheath of worship.

This ceremonial—this sheath of worship—is evidenced in various forms. It is found in the great and appealing dignity and purity of style in which the Scriptures are verbally clothed; it is found in characteristic and predisposing architecture consecrated to religious worship; it is seen in that decorum in which religious exercises are conducted. It should also be found in that other great art which may most intimately express and impressively embody the religious spirit—church music. Much may be gained in religious realization from the ceremonial quality at once inherent in religion and worship and potentially within the power of the arts. The spirit and character of genuine church music should be at one with the dignity of the style of the Scriptures and the uplifting influence of church

10

architecture. A perception of the ceremonial element in religion and all genuinely religious art is of the greatest assistance in helping us to get our bearings and in forming right ideals and judgments in church music. It is the great glory of genuine church music that worship may find in it the mood which is consonant with this ceremonial element in religion, a mood which may awaken, express, and embody the religious. The function of church music in its ceremonial aspect is to be realized by several means: by the pervading atmosphere of the musical composition, by the spirit of its performance, and by that devotional significance which the musical parts are enabled to attain through their relation to the other parts of the service.

THE THREE factors just mentioned—the musical, the conceptual, and the ceremonial—are constituent elements in church music. The fourth factor, the associational, is derivative, coming from the others. It may be either a present, or concurrent, association, or a recall association.

Concurrent-association is to be found in physical surroundings, such as ecclesiastical architecture, which has conceptual and ceremonial suggestiveness and in the demeanor appropriate to the conduct of public worship. These stimulate the conceptual and ceremonial elements and should be recognized and accredited as factors in church music. The art of music in religious worship should not be isolated and separated from its proper associates. Music combines more freely with its sister arts, and also with many of man's activities, than any other of the fine arts. On this account, it is perhaps the most elusive. Conceptual and ceremonial factors in the church service which are in fields other than the musical are properly to be called upon to enhance the effectiveness of church music. The employment of these concurrent-associational factors, intelligently treated, fosters and enlarges the influence of church music.

More powerful, and more elusive perhaps than the influence of the concurrent-associational factor in church music is the

11

recall-associational. We worship under the impress of manifold past religious experiences. Church music, intensifying religious consciousness and holding it in memorable form, is a potent means of reviving it. We constantly live with and add to our past experience. Through its revival and recollection our present religious emotion is proof positive of its enduring character. It is evident that we acquire a fund of experience which is not ephemeral, but permanent and cumulative. Though this may not remain at white heat, it has permanency. Our emotional and attitudinal life below the level of consciousness is large. When music in religious worship stirs it so that our religious selves rise to clear consciousness, we are amazed at its power, and perhaps surprised at its existence. It is strong, invigorating, sustaining, extremely subtle and complex. It draws upon a vast and varied repository.

The great force of the associational-recall factor in church music is seen in the enormous influence which "old favorites" commonly possess. These often have a strength out of all proportion to their merit. So it is that much music of indifferent quality is continued in use because of its sacred association. Association exercises a very strong influence on the affections. Sacred associations gather around what we sing or hear sung in church so that, for the individual, petty music often becomes effective church music—effective in that with its use one's soul wakens, is stirred and brought to greater spiritual consciousness and activity. Memories of the highest order cluster about and animate such familiar music, bringing refreshment and inspiration through the subtle power of recall-association.

But the recall-associational factor in church music, important and valuable as it is, is often too much relied upon. Its strength is sometimes so great that it is taken to be the all-important thing. Its power is so subtle, its elements are so mixed, it is so confusing and bewildering, that it tends to becloud the original, constituent elements in church music, and cause neglect of the study and development of these basic factors. The recall-associational factor should be utilized, but this should be done intelligently and constructively.

Awareness of its great influence should make us constantly mindful that we are ever creating the recall material of the future, that the associations of tomorrow are being created today. This fact is an incentive to making the church music of today as worthy and as appropriate as possible both for the effectiveness of its present use and for its future influence. By improving the quality of present practice in church music, we are not only avoiding stagnation in the present but also are preparing a richer store for future recall.

It should be noted that in this subjective recall effected in church music, it is the religious element which is in the ascendancy and not the musical, for in this resurgence it is the religious rather than the purely musical which comes back with special force. And it should be noted that the recall-association more than the concurrent-association is personal and individual; like our nervous system, it is extremely sensitive, deeply embedded, and very far-reaching.

These four factors—the musical, the conceptual, the ceremonial, and the associational—are present in varying qualities and in varying proportions in all church music, from the music of the Salvation Army to that of the grandest cathedral service. The strands of the various factors are generally more or less distinct, though the fibres of which they are composed may not be disentangled and isolated—but this is not necessary.

The best church music is that in which all these factors are present in their most exalted and efficient form. The vision of such an ideal is illuminating. By clearly perceiving the various factors and understanding more and more their nature and worth, we may make substantial progress in church music. Each may be considered and improved by itself and in its relation to the others. All of them, as they exist in our present practice, are capable of being modified. By keeping them carefully in mind one becomes more alert and discerning; and the problem becomes clearer, more interesting, more alive.

CHAPTER III

THE PRACTICE OF CHURCH MUSIC

A CORRECT CONCEPTION of the nature and function of church music is not all that is requisite for the attainment of genuine church music. Besides a clear ideal and a sound theory, there must be an effective practice. It is one thing to perceive the purpose of church music, and quite another to attain it.

At closest range, church music is ever a practical problem. Services are of such frequent occurrence, the use of music in them is so considerable and the means and resources are so limited, that the concrete task of securing some music or other for immediate use is always likely to be pressing. Something must be had and this immediately, with all too little opportunity for improvement in the character and effectiveness of the music. Often the office of church musicians is taken to be that of providing music which conforms to traditional procedure or stereotyped current custom—no matter how dull and ineffective it may be. Generally this is the only thing expected by the church; sometimes, it is the only thing permitted.

All blame for the music of the church not being really valuable cannot be laid at the door of the church musician. Neither can it be laid to the charge of the minister or the congregation, although they, as well as the church musicians, have a large responsibility in the matter. Much of the ineffectualness of church music, an important part, is the fault of the system current in our churches. Policies and practices are to a large extent defective or deficient. There is an absence of a clear and guiding concept as to the essential purpose of church music and failure to adopt the best and most practical methods of attainment. Attempts are indeed made every now and then to effect improvement, but instead of attention and energies being devoted to the essential problem of ensuring genuine church music, the real problem is often dodged. A panacea is sought—subterfuges are resorted to: a new hymn book is adopted; the choir is abolished in the hope of improving congregational singing; or a choir is started to stimulate the music of the church; the music of the regular services is neglected in order to develop special ones; or again, pageants are worked up and featured. The high use of music in religious worship is not made central. Instead, there is much petty, sentimental, or sensational use of music. As a result, church music is ineffective and little esteemed; it does not have the full respect of those in the pews, nor is it of such a quality religiously and musically as to enlist interest to the extent that it should and secure the devotion of church members and competent musicians.

Discussions of church music and attempts to improve it are often fruitless because adequate attention is not given to both theory and practice, and because consideration is not thorough-going. In the theory of church music actual conditions and the requisites for successful achievement are not duly considered, while in the practice its purpose is not given adequate attention and the best methods of attainment are not sufficiently utilized.

As THE designation implies, church music is a dual subject. It is at once a special and restricted field in the domain of musical art and a special and restricted field in the realm of religion. In the religious realm it has two phases: one purely religious and non-musical, the other having musical reference. The first of these involves such matters as the constitution of the textual substance of the service, its arrangement, and the ceremonial conduct of services—all of which, in furnishing a religious basis and atmosphere, affect church music; the second has to do with the suitability of particular liturgical material for musical expression. Likewise in the domain of music, there are two distinct phases: one involving questions of the proper character of music for use in religious services and the right spirit of performance; the second having to do with musical technique and practical management.

Many of these matters which are of fundamental importance in the practice of church music lie in highly specialized and technical departments of religion and music. For the benefit of the church at large, these should be treated by persons who are particularly competent in these fields. On the religious side material which is obsolete should be supplanted by that which is vital and inspiring; suggestions should be made indicating how both congregational and choir music may be given settings in the service which will allow them to be not merely logically and esthetically correct, but religiously vital. And on the musical side, technical points and practical methods which would enhance the music of the church, both as pure music and as church music, should be made available to choir workers so that wasteful and bungling methods may be avoided and church music become what it should be in religious worship.

CHURCH MUSIC is an applied art. That it is an applied art and not a free art might at first seem to lead to the conclusion that it is an inferior art, possibly a degraded form of art. But when one considers that religion supplies the most sublime and profound subjects for musical expression and that it stirs incentives to devotional expression, then it is clear that its association with religion properly exalts church music. Its unique function may be realized with music of humble form, as in the simplest chant or hymn tune, or with music of great elaboration, as in the Sanctus of the B minor mass of Bach. Whether in humble or elaborate expression, music allied to religious thought and emotion may be an exalted and profoundly moving art.

Being an applied art, church music is in its practice necessarily a matter of adaptation. Therein is one of its greatest difficulties, for no two churches have music problems that are exactly alike. There are endless degrees of differences. Nevertheless, situations tend to resolve themselves into general types, based on differing religious aims and methods, and on musical considerations, such as the general church-music tradition of the given church, its musical resources, and the musical responsiveness of the congregation.

Things which are secondary in church music should be kept distinct from those which are primary. Secondary phases and aspects are numerous, and some of them have a way of forcing themselves into the foremost place. Often they are made central. Take, for example, schools of church music—the Gregorian, Anglican, Russian, the evangelistic. The outcome of different histories and ruling ideas, these different kinds of church music are more or less distinctly appropriate to and related to the different types of Christian worship from which they have evolved, for they have grown out of the needs which they serve. In practice each church should adopt that procedure which is best suited to itself, and this should be made as effective as possible. Consideration of religious effectiveness should be the criterion of selection and not mere desire for uniformity.

AT THE VERY OUTSET it is wise to eliminate one source of much misdirected effort and much ineffective church music, and that is over-elaboration. The matter of elaboration is, at most, of secondary importance, and hardly that. Often it is pressed into the first place, causing much confusion and trouble. The tendency towards too great elaboration is a common weakness, occasioned on the one hand by misplaced ambition of church musicians and on the other by the demands of their employers, the music committee and the congregation. As the church is musically a heterogeneous body, it is obvious that in church music the less degree of complication consistent with the attainment of its function the better. Elaboration is not in itself an excellence in church music; in fact, it is quite likely to be the reverse. The tendency to elaboration is largely due to the idea that there should be one standard of church music, which in turn comes from failure to perceive and take into account the difference between ideal and standard. This error is seen in small struggling churches attempting to provide the same musical procedure and practice as the largest. The problem of elaboration is one of adjustment to conditions, not one of ideal of church music.

But though elaboration is a secondary matter, it is nevertheless not an unimportant one. Expression in religious worship should be the best possible. There is of course the danger of paying too much regard to means and manner and too little to the essential character of worship; but this danger does not justify disregard of the matter of investiture. First of all, and above all, there should be constant regard for sincerity.

MUSICALLY, churches fall into three classes: those having meagre musical resources and capabilities; those in which the musical resources and capabilities are considerable but not extensive; and those in which they are abundant. In the first of these, the music should be of the simplest sort; in the second class both choir and organ music are used in making the service effective through employment of the art of music; while in the third class the fullest use of music appropriate to worship is possible.

The first should properly be larger than it is. In many churches there is mere aping, the appointment of a choir being taken for granted as a musical advance, little or no regard being given to the consideration as to whether or not the choir will be of value in the service. Whatever is undertaken should be made to have devotional dignity and bring inspiration. A simple service may be profoundly impressive. Many churches should limit themselves entirely to congregational music. Yet wherever possible there should be some sort of a vocal nucleus to lead in congregational singing and assist in making it effective. In order to maintain such a group it may be advisable to have them occasionally emerge as a choir singing some simple music; but to give them a regular and considerable place in the service, whether or no, is unwise. The extent and frequency of their singing as a separate body is obviously a matter to be determined with discretion and tact.

A large number of churches belong in the second class. Here there may be considerable choir music. Whatever its amount or degree of elaboration, it should be pertinent and adequately performed. Elaborate music should be undertaken only when it is certain that the given composition is desirable church music and that it will be worthily rendered in the service. A choir should never seem to be feeling its way through a hymn or response or felt to be struggling through an anthem. In some churches there is overmuch choir music, often tediously extensive and poorly performed. Fewer or shorter choir numbers, as the case may be, would in many instances be more effective.

The number of churches forming the third class will be comparatively small. With their ample resources, churches of this class may be able to attain the fullest and most elaborate achievement in church music. They may set forth most gloriously the high service of music in religious worship. But they have their temptations, and like others, are in danger of miscarrying and failing in essentials. Their opportunities are great; so also, are their responsibilities. Others look up to them, as to a big brother, for their ideals. The spirit and character of the music in these churches should be such as to guide and stimulate others.

Few churches may properly aspire to the richest and most elaborate style of church music, but when it is realized that the great ideal may be held by all—and that every individual will probably have his limitations of one sort or another, and that only partial attainment is possible—each may feel a satisfaction in that so far as his conditions admit, he has been able to realize that which is substantial, genuine, and of the highest quality. We may all share in the great ideal, even though we are not privileged to have perfect conditions and perfect material to work with.

MUSIC IN WORSHIP

THE ATTAINMENT of genuine church music is not, as is commonly and erroneously thought, a matter pertaining only to church musicians. Music, it is true, is created by the musician; but in the development of good church music clergy and congregation, as well as church musicians, have part, each in his own way. When worship—adoration, divine consciousness and aspiration—are made central, then it is seen that the congregation, clergy, and choir are on the same plane, clergy and choir being merely leaders. Together they constitute a body of worshipers, all of whom have to do, in one way or another, with music in the church service.

For the full attainment of the function of music in promoting and elevating worship education is needful. This may come through instruction and elucidation and through experience in worship. The church owes it to itself to see to it that its worship is the noblest and most sincere possible.

CLEARLY there are two general areas in the practice of church music: first an area subject to general principles and rules—matters of correct ideal, vital liturgical substance, effective procedure, appropriate and feasible music, competent musical technique; and second, an area of activity, inevitably variable and more or less indeterminate in character, having to do with matters of detail which can be effectively treated only in their individual setting and by those in charge. It is wise to segregate as much as possible the permanent and definite elements in order to develop the best procedure and practice. If this is done, church music will undoubtedly be found to be subject more and more to principle and rule, and the area of the variable and the indeterminate will be reduced.

Though we may expect that as time goes on, church music will increasingly become a matter of principle, it is not to be expected that society will ever be so unified and uniform as to make conditions and situations alike in all places. The conditions of its practice will always be variable and there will always be call for individual discretion and judgment. Far from

20

becoming settled uniformly once and for all, church music problems can never become so, any more than business and educational procedures; but like business and education, church music may be conducted more and more intelligently and successfully. Even so, from its very nature, it will always remain "the everlasting church music problem."

As its theory and practice attain a more substantial basis, church music will assume a larger and more important function in religious worship, and at the same time there will be less tendency to undue elaboration. Unessential musical tasks will be measurably diminished, better and more suitable music will be assured, and greater religious significance be attained. Thereby the function of church music will be more fully realized, and the church service become both more worthy and more inspiring.

CHAPTER IV

TWO FORMS OF GENUINE CHURCH MUSIC

It is the presence of a religious element in church music which differentiates it from music in general and constitutes it church music. Consequently, in church music, the religious element is to be taken as basic, the *sine qua non*. But though the word "religious" may be taken to designate the distinguishing element, religion itself has many phases and aspects. Scholars, in their study of religion, have framed fifty and more definitions of it, and statistical reports of religious bodies in the United States enumerate between one hundred and fifty and two hundred different denominations of "those who profess and call themselves Christians." Thus, instead of simplicity on the religious side of church music, we have complexity—apparently a bewildering complexity. But fortunately, the case is not so bad as it might seem, at least as regards church music, for many of the sects derive their individuality from minor differences, chiefly in matters of theology and church polity. There are, however, a considerable number of denominational families within the church; yet, even here, the case again is not so bad as it might be, for even with all the differences there are in these families—in church ideals and methods, in church-music traditions and in culture and musical facilities—the number of kinds of church music, as based on types of religion and religious services, may be reduced to two orders, which we will designate as "the evangelical" and "the ecclesiastical."

The type of religious service upon which the ecclesiastical order of church music is based and with which it is associated makes a relatively large use of worship, while the evangelical has exhortation and appealing exegesis as distinctive features. Now both worship and exhortation are genuine religious activities, but they are quite different in their use of music. It is through a difference of function which music is called upon to exercise in connection with them that the two types of church music, "the ecclesiastical" and "the evangelical," are created. And it is with regard to this difference, and not with reference to any matters of church polity and theology, that we wish to employ the words "ecclesiastical" and "evangelical" in designating these two orders or uses of church music.

In the ecclesiastical type of religion and church service, it is the universal which is relatively the more prominent; while in the evangelical, it is the particular and individual. In the ecclesiastical there is a strong sense of the cosmic, the historical, the traditional. The ecclesiastical is characteristically reflective, meditative, and naturally quieter; the evangelical more impulsively intense and also more individualistic. In the former there is a strong apprehension of the Eternal and the Fatherhood of God; the spiritual sense is more objectively directed. On the other hand, in the evangelical it is the sense of discipleship, of comradship which is particularly strong. In the ecclesiastical the religious consciousness appears in the reflective form of repentance, aspiration, adoration, communion; while in the evangelical it takes the form of spiritual assurance and the impulse to appeal to one's fellows in their religious behalf. In the one case, the soul approaches the Throne of Divine Grace through worship; in the other the soul is stirred and made keenly conscious by the call of God largely through preaching and exhortation.

CORRESPONDING to these general types of religion and religious services, and due to them, there are two different attitudes to be found within the church at large with regard to the character which church music should have. At the one extreme, are those who would have it formal, reverent, dignified, and in some instances even austere in character; at the other, are those who would have it passionate and impulsive—pathetic, dramatic, pleading, exuberant or it may be sentimental or even merely graceful. The distinctive features of these types are often exaggerated through tradition and accentuated through partisan opposition. Each type has frequently been unduly stressed in practice with resulting ineffectiveness and confusion of thought.

The ecclesiastical order or use of church music, being more reflective than the evangelical, more objective, more detailed, has from the standpoint of art more range, more light and shade, more color, more perspective. In the ecclesiastical type of church service and church music there is greater variety of mood than in the evangelical. Mood, it should be noted, is comparatively qualitative; whereas impulse, which is directly or indirectly characteristic of evangelical church music, is comparatively quantitive rather than qualitative. The use of music is consequentially much more refined and distinctive in worship than in connection with exhortation. The higher qualities of music as a fine art are more available in the ecclesiastical than in the evangelical type.

It is in worship-music that church music finds its highest function and estate. Music which seeks to express religious aspiration and to aid in religious communion will *per se* be more deeply religious in character than that which is used largely to stimulate emotional responsiveness. Being a medium of religious expression and impression, ecclesiastical church music in itself, more than the evangelical, is an embodiment of the religious sense and is more distinctly "religious." So it is that we find that ecclesiastical church music is inherently and inevitably more widely differentiated from secular music than is evangelical.

As church music should be suited to the religious methods of the church employing it, it is seen to be not a unitary, but a dual problem. There are clearly two typical purposes for which music is used in religious services, and these call for music so different in character and operation, in materials and methods as to constitute two orders of church music.

In all church music there is, of course, both a certain

emotional warmth and a certain contemplative element. It is with regard to the relative strength and the character of these, together with the emphasis of the particular function that music is called upon to exercise in the given instance, that the classification "evangelical" and "ecclesiastical" is made. Sometimes the distinctive character of church music in regard to these aspects is pronounced and sometimes it is slight. However it may be, this difference of function which music may have in the service is a matter of fundamental importance in the theory and practice of church music.

In some churches the two types of service and of church music are to be found together, a stately ecclesiastical service in the morning and a distinctly informal, perhaps an evangelistic or semi-evangelistic, service in the evening. In many instances, moreover, the two orders of church music, but not of course in their extreme forms, may be found mingled in a single service, the music in the earlier part of the service being of the more ecclesiastical sort, while in the latter part of the service, in places just before or after the sermon, the music may be of rather the evangelical sort. Yet, despite these facts, the two orders of church music should always be kept distinct in one's mind. Otherwise there is likely to be more or less inappropriateness and ineffectiveness in the music of the particular church, together with waste of both time and effort.

The ecclesiastical order of church music, in that it is the more intimately associated with the definitely religious, is the superior form of genuine church music on its religious side, and since it makes fuller and finer use of the art of music for religious expressiveness, it is also the superior form of church music on the musical side. In drawing the distinction between the ecclesiastical and the evangelical, the purpose has been to disclose the fact that there are two typical religious bases to which music finds itself related in its service for religion and that these constitute two distinct uses of music. In the consideration of this matter, it has not been the intention to discredit that type of religion or of church service which does

25

not demand of music the most distinctive service it can render; nor has it been the intention to extol that type which affords opportunity for the highest use of music just because it does afford that opportunity.

INASMUCH as it is in the ecclesiastical order of church music that the art of church music finds its highest and most distinctive service, we have taken the ecclesiastical type of church service and the ecclesiastical order of church music as the basis of our consideration of the subject. This highest and unique use should be cultivated as far as possible, both for itself and because, through its influence, it will tend to improve the less distinctive use, infusing into it more vitality than it otherwise might have. The influence of ecclesiastical church music may be valuable in promoting the evangelical, whereas the evangelical type has comparatively little to offer for the ecclesiastical.

The recent efforts to improve services through the addition of ritualistic items, together with an increased use of music in them, indicates a craving for more of the worshipful in our services generally. This movement, however, has often been blind, bungling and ineffectual. Plea for the ecclesiastical type and use of church music may properly be made both because of the inherent value of worship and also, pardonably on the part of the church musician, because of the desirability of securing for music the highest value in the service of religion.

As the emphasis on the ecclesiastical or evangelical basis which church music serves is different in individual churches and in various groups of churches, there will probably ever be varied types of church music, ranging from that appropriate to the ultra ecclesiastical to that appropriate to the ultra evangelical, that is to say the evangelistic type of service. Adjustment of type of church music to type of religious service is most important, and should be effected intelligently and carefully. With greater regard for the element of worship in the modern church service, proper attention to this matter will undoubtedly bring about a more extensive adoption of the ecclesiastical use of church music.

Both the evangelical and the ecclesiastical are orders of genuine church music, for in them its ideal is realized. In each its function may be attained—that of bringing to stronger and clearer consciousness our distinctly religious nature, our high spiritual character and destiny. But, though the goal may be reached by both, the manner and means whereby this is attained will differ to such an extent and so fundamentally, at least in the more extreme instances, as to constitute two forms of genuine church music.

CHAPTER V

CHURCH MUSIC VERSUS MUSIC IN CHURCH

To ONE scrutinizing the use of music in religious services it is obvious that it is employed in distinctly different ways. On the one hand, it is used to serve as an attraction or diversion, to afford musical pleasure and satisfaction of one sort or another; and on the other hand, to aid in religious expression and impression. In the one case we have "music in church," in the other genuine "church music."

As has already been said, it is the presence of a religious element which differentiates church music from music in general and constitutes it specifically church music. This element, it will be recalled, may be present in various ways: directly, in more or less definite religious thought; or indirectly, by means of the ceremonial factor expressing this, or through the power of associational recall, or, again, through the influence of concurrent association, such, for instance, as ecclesiastical architecture may exert.

By its giving added expressiveness to the religious, genuine church music becomes an integral part of the service. "Music in church," on the contrary, being at best a religiously superficial attraction, is not an organic part of the service, but rather something incidental.

The distinction between "church music" and "music in church" is one of function and not one of label. It is not, as is quite commonly assumed, a matter of this or that musical composition being "sacred" or otherwise. It may not always be possible to find clear demarcation, but the two uses or orders can nevertheless generally be perceived and distinguished. The distinction is fundamentally a self-evident one, a distinction of function realized in experience.

CHURCH MUSIC VERSUS MUSIC IN CHURCH

In genuine church music the musical, through its power of expression and impression, exalts the religious, stimulating and clarifying religious consciousness. Church music exists for this purpose; it must function religiously. When the music of the church fails to do so, it ceases to be bona fide church music and becomes "music in church."

BOTH RELIGION and music are complex experiences; each has many phases. Obviously, their interaction and interrelation in church music is not a simple matter. In genuine church music the musical is properly subservient to the religious. This does not mean that the function of the musical is not an exalted one, or that its status is not a truly honorable one. Quite the reverse, especially in the ecclesiastical use of church music. The loftier and more inherently distinctive the religious, the higher the office of church music.

The religious influence of music in the church service may be strong and significantly expressive, or it may be weak and inconsequential. Music may deepen the religious sense and purpose of the service, or it may become a centre of attraction, absorbing attention to itself.

Unlike architecture, music is not a static art. Existing in the realm of time, it has ever to be re-created. And worship also, at least for most mortals, has ever to be renewed or re-enacted. Since this is so, it is not to be expected that the religious and the musical elements will be constantly of the same relative force. There will be fluctuation. Perhaps only seldom will there be absolute constancy in the attainment of genuine church music as against "music in church." The proper ascendancy of the religious cannot be guaranteed, but much may be done to secure it. Consciousness and consideration of the distinction between genuine church music and "music in church" is a great and constant aid.

Church music is personal in its functioning, and on this account, will not in every respect be the same for all. Responsiveness varies in individuals. The same music may meet with different responses in different persons; indeed, response may be different for the same person at different times and in different conditions. Church music, like other human experience, is therefore likely to be in a state of flux. "Music in church" and "church music" are often intermittent in one's experience, not uniform and constant; as a matter of fact, they occasionally shade off from one to the other. Nevertheless, the realization of genuine church music is not so fugitive and elusive that intelligent treatment of the matter may not reasonably be counted to attain it.

It should also be pointed out that responsiveness will, in general, vary with different cultural groups. The degree in which the purely musical factor in church music may act in disposing to worship is dependent upon one's particular cultural and musical background and his environment. The enjoyment of beautiful, serene music may be religiously fruitful, or it may not. That depends upon the background against which it happens to be placed. For those whose surroundings in life are rude and dingy, devoid of external beauty, simple beautiful music, taking them into new realms, may have a transforming radiance, elevating and refreshing—disposing to worship. What for some might ordinarily be "music in church" may for others become genuine church music.

To draw a sharp division between the musically aesthetic and emotional and the religious in our mental and spiritual life is impossible. Do we not speak of "the beauty of holiness"? But though we may speak of one in terms of the other, though they arise and exist in the same side of our being, they are nevertheless not identical. The realms of the religious and the musical are in many ways different in character; yet in certain areas they have somewhat in common. Were it not for this fact, music would not have been persistently and intimately associated with the religious throughout the ages. It is on this account that music is capable of being an aid to religion.

The issue of "music in church" versus "church music" is one of long standing: Saint Augustine, in the year 397 A.D., wrote:

CHURCH MUSIC VERSUS MUSIC IN CHURCH

"When it befalls me to be more moved with the voice than with the words sung, I confess to have sinned."

How THE MUSIC of the church is to be made genuine church music and not remain merely "music in church" is the great central problem. Of the two elements in church music, the musical and the religious, the religious is the one to which we must look for the distinctive feature which differentiates it from secular music. This element is found in the conceptual, the ceremonial and the associational factors, as these have been defined in Chapter II. The musical factor, however, has an important role. The character of the musical composition and the spirit of its performance have their part in the creation of genuine church music.

Music, adequately performed, possesses to a marked degree a character of its own; it may arouse a mood of its own making. Music itself may have a definite emotional character. Because of this a piece of music may be described as tender, triumphant, yearning, confident, mournful, joyous, filled with hope, reverent, mystical. Now as religious worship, by its very nature, has distinctive character and mood, we may properly designate as religious such music as may induce a corresponding mood. Unfortunately, a great deal of the music heard in churches is emotionally nondescript and not of a character ideally to be called "religious." There is, however, music which can be so called. As we may properly speak of some music as theatrical, as dramatic, and so forth, so we may designate other music, such as is in accord with the mood and spirit of religious worship, as churchly or religious.

Music may express what words cannot. We all know that words sung are different from words spoken. If rightly used, music may greatly enhance religious expression. Indeed, as Frazer in *The Golden Bough* has pointed out, music, "the most intimate and affecting of the arts, has done much to create as well as to express the religious emotions, thus modifying more or less deeply the fabric to which at first sight it seems only to

31

minister." The religiously conceptual element may be transmitted to the music by way of the associational and ceremonial factors.

THERE are many influences which naturally favor the attainment of genuine church music. Among them is a realization of the true character and significance of divine worship; consciousness of the church service as a supreme occasion; regard for the church building as a sanctuary; a spirit of performance in the music which is in accord with that of religious worship; and finally the character of the church service itself, its substance, its construction, and its conduct.

One of the most important of these means of securing the requisite religious element in church music is by duly magnifying the exaltedness of the church service. The fact that intrinsically the church service—divine worship—is a great and sublime occasion should be made central, an occasion suffused with the loftiest, most intimate and inspiring religious and ethical spirit. The service of worship should be clothed with proper ceremonial and its sublimity expressed in the most significant and appropriate music. Pertinent ceremonial and music are normal aids, dependable and constituent. The sense of religious occasion, properly magnified in its inherent character, greatly aids music in realizing its high function in the service of religion.

Furthermore, the sense of special occasion in religious services is of very great power. In the Roman church it is implicit in the mass, where it is tremendous. In the Protestant church its power is recognized and attempts are made to create it—sermon topics are advertised, special musical programs are announced, this and that group is specially addressed, various anniversaries are celebrated. But though the influence of special occasion is recognized, it is often only superficially used. It is not sufficiently realized that its legitimate value is resident in the profoundly religious nature of the occasion.

In passing, it should perhaps be noted that in certain situations, as for example at a funeral or at one of the great Christian festivals, there is an over-powering presence of the religiously conceptual so that it may happen that the influence of music is very slight except on the lower planes of physical and crudely emotional stimulation. The poorest and most superficial music may then appear to be exalted, borne aloft on the wings of the religious intensity of the occasion. In such circumstances the higher musical function, the quality of the music, its mood and performance, may appear inconsequential and negligible, and the status of church music and the office of the church musician may appear correspondingly inferior and inconsiderable. In fact, in such circumstances the art of church music is practically dispensed with. This is not a normal condition, and it should not be taken as such.

The influence of place of worship is also an important aid to the attainment of genuine church music. As the house we live in becomes a home, so the place in which we worship—in which others, it may have been for generations, have worshiped —becomes a sanctuary, a sanctuary in the etymological sense of that word. Whether the church building is consecrated by hands or not, it is consecrated by the holy aspirations, the comfort and solace, the heavenly visions and satisfactions which have been experienced there. A place set apart, where the trivial, the fleeting, and the short-sighted give place to the enduring, the ennobling, and the inspiring, where distraction and disappointment are changed into serenity and hope, the church becomes a sacred place—in truth, the House of God. The religious character of the building may be enhanced by the arts. Architecture may impart the sense of dignity, of permanency, of grandeur and majesty, while music, through the rarer atmosphere it can create, may bring to stronger consciousness the high and holy things of the spirit. With such a concept before the church musician and the worshiper, genuine church music may be more readily possible of attainment. "Music in church" will then seem out of place; it may even seem profane and vulgar. The sense and mood of worship is greatly increased by one's considering the church as a place of consecration.

MUSIC IN WORSHIP

The designation and setting apart of a stated time for the church service is another important influence affecting the character of the service and the effectiveness of music in it. The fact that religious services are definitely and regularly placed as to time is something more than a matter of practical arrangement. A stated time set apart, like a place set apart, is not only appropriate, but intrinsically conducive to religious worship. It is in consonance with the act of worship, deliberate and purposive, not casual and incidental. The church service is a comparatively short period regularly reserved for the nurture and growth of our higher selves. In every way it should be most carefully constituted and effectively conducted. Carelessness, unpreparedness, inadequacy or triviality here is most reprehensible. The quality and value of the service is largely in the keeping of the minister and the church musicians. For them to provide for this period less than that which is most valuable and pertinent, at whatever cost, constitutes by so much failure in their high calling and duty. Theirs is much more than an opportunity; it is an obligation. When a church musician, without sanctimoniousness, is conscious of the high character of the service he should render, he will the more readily distinguish between what is "church music" and what is "music in church." And not only on the part of the clergy and the church musicians but also on the part of the congregation, the consciousness of the high purpose and sacredness of the hour of worship is an important aid in the attainment of genuine church music.

UNLIKE all the other arts, except the drama, music is constitutionally in need of an intermediary between the one who originally conceived it and the one to whom it makes appeal. Music has ever to be re-created. Between composer and auditor is the performer, whose task is not merely that of mechanically putting together a work of art: his function is that of a re-creating, vitalizing interpreter. In church music much depends upon the spirit of performance. This is directly dependent upon the individual church musicians, and has a great deal to do with determining whether we have church music or merely music in church.

The spirit of performance of music in the church may be deeply devotional and religious in character, or it may be secular and religiously unsignificant. Solos are frequently surcharged with false pathos and suffused with weak sentiment; choir music is often highly sensitized, exuberant, and explosive; and congregational music, too, is often devoid of devotional animation. A right spirit in performance is as essential as right notes.

What then should be the spirit of performance in church music? As worship has distinctive and characteristic mood—and it is the function of church music to embody and intensify this—the character of church music and the spirit of its performance, which is a part of it, should be in consonance with the general mood of worship. Within the church there properly and significantly reigns a spirit and mood quite different from that of the world outside. Inevitably the solemn sense of the Presence of God, uplifting and ennobling, and possessing a certain mystical quality, creates a consciousness distinctly different from that consciousness and spirit which we call secular. But the dignity and solemnity of the sacred and religious is not properly mournful and depressing; on the contrary, it is exalting and inspiring. In church music, as in worship, there should be joy and confidence, rapture, aspiration, poise and earnestness.

The proper model for the style of church music, both in its composition and in its performance, is to be found in the expression of thought and emotion in the Holy Scriptures. Naturally religious music should have the same general character as religious literature. In expression as well as in substance the Holy Scriptures are unique and invaluable. In them there is nothing bombastic, nothing blatant, nothing filled with frigid awe; and on the other hand, there is nothing sentimental or mawkish, nothing cringing, nothing hysterical. In tone and temper of expression the Scriptures—especially as found in the King James translation, characterized by Professor John Livingston Lowes of Harvard as "the noblest monument of English prose"—affords guidance for those charged with the conduct of church music.

OTHER INFLUENCES affecting the attainment of genuine church music are to be found in the personal attitudes towards worship and church music on the part of church musicians, ministers and the congregation.

In the performance of church music the individuality of the musician should be lost in the function of his office. Church musicians should not stand forth and be unduly prominent either as individuals or as groups. They are simply leaders or agents in worship. It is, of course, possible that the presence of certain ones in the choir—like the daughter of Longfellow's Village Blacksmith, whose voice recalled the mother—may enhance religious appeal for a particular person, but this is of exceptional occurrence. The congregation, clergy and choir constitute a body of worshipers. As the individuality of those in the pews is submerged and effaced in the act of worship, so also should be the individuality of those in the choir seats. To intrude one's personality is out of place in divine worship.

As the minister and the musicians share in the conduct of worship, and as their respective parts are often alternating and should be vitally correlated, the minister is an important participant in the attainment of genuine church music. The devotional spirit should possess minister and choir. Their offices are allied. Genuine church music is made difficult of attainment for the church musicians, sometimes impossible, when the clerical parts intervening between or adjacent to the musical are perfunctory and unrelated. Some ministers seem to be strangely unfamiliar with or indifferent to this part of the service—at least it sometimes appears so from the pews and from the organ bench. Most ministers, however, are effective in this matter, some pre-eminently so.

CHURCH MUSIC VERSUS MUSIC IN CHURCH

The members of the congregation also have an important part in the achievement of genuine church music. Their conception of the service, their conduct, and their attitude towards its musical parts are matters of essential influence. In fact, they create conditions favorable or unfavorable to their own realization of genuine church music, and these conditions in turn react on the church musicians, affecting their office and their service.

Finally, there is the service, its textual substance, its arrangement, and its conduct. This is a matter of very great importance in securing the religious element in church music and will be considered in the two following chapters.

CHAPTER VI

MUSIC AND THE CHURCH SERVICE

THE SERVICE is the great source from which the religious element in church music is derived and by which it is maintained. It is largely by the thoughts, conceptions, and emotional attitude aroused through the use of language that we secure the conceptual factor, which, in one form or another, is essential in worship and church music.

From the earliest days vocal music—language and music in conjunction—has been characteristic of Christianity. It has ever been, and still is, the basic music of the Christian church. Instrumental music, to be sure, has been cultivated and put to good use, especially in modern times, but it has always been secondary. Vocal music has ever predominated. This has been so not only because it is more available, but also because it is more apt and generally more potent. In vocal music we have words and music in combination, two arts each of which may give distinctive expressiveness and embodiment to religious thought and emotion. In this union the words, being more definite and directive, are the more fundamental feature. Hence it is that in the theory and practice of church music, consideration of the church service as a means of attaining genuine church music is very important.

In the study and practice of church music it is ever to be borne in mind that the purpose of the service and that of religious music are one and the same—to enhance and nourish our religious life; also, that religion is inevitably more comprehensive than the church, the church than the church service, and the church service than church music.

The textual substance of the service is important both for

the service and for church music. If it is vital, music is afforded an exalted field of expression, attention to music for itself will tend to be forestalled, and we shall have genuine church music rather than merely music in church. The purpose for which music has been admitted into the sanctuary largely rests upon and is related to the substance and conduct of the service.

THERE ARE COMMONLY considered to be two types of church services: the ritualistic or liturgical, and the non-ritualistic or non-liturgical. This classification is quite general and not so discerningly critical as may most profitably be made. By means of more detailed and critical discriminations among types of church services the problem of its influence and function in the field of church music may be greatly clarified. In place of the two commonly recognized types, the ritualistic or liturgical, and the non-ritualistic or non-liturgical, there may be seen to be, either in current use or advantageously available, four distinct types of church services.

The words "ritual" and "liturgy" are commonly used as synonyms. In technical theological language, however, they are given certain specific meanings—the word "liturgy," for instance, in the Anglican Communion is used primarily as pertaining to the Eucharist. In contrast with these, it is possible, for purposes of considering church music and its relation to the church service, to give to these words other and special meanings whereby a source of misconception and blundering in the domain of church music may be detected and a means of attaining a sound and substantial basis of improvement be disclosed.

THE WORDS "ritual" and "liturgy" may properly be used to designate two quite different things. A "ritual" involves a rite, an act according to a formula; a rite involves authority; and authority must be vested in a priesthood. The word "liturgy," on the other hand, may be used to designate merely an ordered service, a service the substance of which has been selected and agreed upon for purposes of common worship by those engaging in the worship. When the Protestant churches, with the exception of some like the Anglicans and Lutherans, threw over ecclesiasticism, they threw away ritual and liturgy as being one and the same thing, not seeing that they were not necessarily identical; and in place of ritual and liturgy—since some service plan is necessary in concerted worship—they devised what has come to be known as The Order of Worship.

The use of the word "liturgy" to designate a body of devotional material selected and agreed upon for purpose of common worship, but without any ritualistic implications attached to it, affords a means of making important distinction among services collectively and indiscriminatingly known as "ritualistic" and "liturgical." It furthermore enables us to conceive a type of service which, while not including any ritualistic ideas, will make available for Protestant churches the strength and value of what we specifically designate the "liturgical" principle.

The essential feature of ritualism, so far as the structure and conduct of the service itself is concerned, is the exact repetition of a formula—a certain efficacious substance used in a certain order by an apostolically authorized person. Obviously this requires the use of a single service structure and substance for a specific given purpose, and entails repetition. But although the idea of liturgy is associated with that of ritual, it may be separated from it and made the basis of a distinct procedure. The liturgical principle may be used without any ritualistic implications: a service may be constituted of a substance and have a general structure which is agreed upon beforehand by those using it as a means and medium of worship without its having any ritualistic assumptions or associations. Such a purely liturgical service may be designated a free-liturgical service.

It should, however, be said that the distinction between ritual and liturgy, though valuable with regard to the structure and character of religious services, is too incisive to be applied rigidly. This is evident if the difference is stated as that between the sacerdotal and the devotional. Almost every religious group has something of both. In fact, they grew up together and both persist in one form or other. The Presbyterians and Baptists, for instance, who would ordinarily not be considered as "sacerdotal," are sacerdotal to the extent that their ministers are "ordained" and specially commissioned to perform the rite of baptism, of communion and of pronouncing a benediction. And on the other hand, in the Roman church devotional exercises, especially private devotional exercises, are important features. The distinction between ritual and liturgy is, nevertheless, fundamentally important as affecting the church service and church music.

By THIS differentiation of the words ritual and liturgy four distinct types of service are disclosed: first, the strictly ritualistic service of the Roman church; second, the ritualistic-liturgical service of the Anglican church; third, the Order of Service, commonly used by most of the various Protestant denominations; and fourth, what may be considered to be a new type of service, conceivable through the designation of the word liturgical entirely devoid of any strictly ritualistic implications—the Free-liturgical Service.

In the first of these, the strictly ritualistic, music is synchronized with the ritualistic action, adding to its expressiveness and enforcing its significance. This use of music will naturally in large measure be different from that in which there is no ritualistic action, and because of this difference in use the problems of music in non-ritualistic services will not be the same as those in the ritualistic service. Each use may be valid for its purpose. In our study of church music we have taken non-ritualistic worship as our basis.

THE SECOND type of service, the ritualistic-liturgical, employs the liturgical principle with ritualistic restriction though not necessarily with ritualistic implications. Emphasis on these latter is more or less varied, but by all using this type of service, both high and low church, ritualistic regularity, due to ritualistic restriction, is in large measure retained. The high church section regards ritualistic implications as valid, whereas the low church section treats ritualistic convention as a tradition. The two sections use the same procedure, but with different significance. The employment of ritualistic restrictions where it is without ritualistic implication seems a hampering tradition. Indeed, this is found to be so by many of those using this type of service, for with them there seems to be increasingly a breaking away from the exactions imposed by strictly ritualistic considerations. The ritualistic features are vital to that section of the church which is ritualistically inclined, but not, at least to the same extent and in the same manner, for those who regard the substance of the service rather as admirable tradition. The liturgical principle embodied in this type of service has much to suggest for attaining vitality in services which are wholly devoid of any ritualistic assumption.

In services of this order, as for example in the Anglican, there is, except in the baptismal and eucharistic sections, a considerable body of distinctly liturgical material which may be freely varied. This, however, is less in the musical than in the clerical parts. In Morning Prayer, for instance, though there are options—the *Te Deum, Benedictus es,* and *Benedicite* after the first lesson, and the *Benedictus* or the *Jubilate* after the second lesson—there is really not a large range of liturgical material. As these canticles, together with the *Venite,* which has no alternate, are rubrical, there is little opportunity in the musical parts of the service for the use of a varied and widely comprehensive body of material. It might, of course, be said that variety and comprehensiveness are provided by the chanting or reading of the Psalms, which, with options in selection, is prescribed. Nevertheless, the musical parts of the service seem, at least to some, to be restricted and conventionally insistent. But even so, the procedure has the merit of affording no room for the cheap and the unworthy. The truth is that almost all the liturgical material in the Anglican service which is designated for musical setting is supremely good; its constant use, however, precludes other material equally good.

THE THIRD type of service is the Order of Service, the type used by most non-ritualistic and non-liturgical churches. Each church plans its own services, both as to form and substance. But though the services are freely and independently constituted by the individual churches, this practice has developed a general type of procedure. This comes from the fact that the several elements in religious worship—prayer, praise, instruction and exhortation—are naturally more or less sequentially related. Habit, moreover, is a stabilizing influence. Then again, the personal limitations of those planning and conducting such services induce conformity to what has become current custom. So it is that the framework of the service tends to have a generally uniform and constant character, while the material used by the individual church is in large measure varied each week. Save for only a few liturgical items such as the Doxology and Lord's Prayer, there is little which one attending a non-liturgical church may definitely expect to find in the service on a Sunday morning.

In the order of service there are two distinct sections: what is generally called the "opening" or "preliminary" exercises, and the sermon. The composition of the first part, in which music has place, and also its relation to the sermonic period should come under consideration in a study of church music.

The order of service has attained its present form and character in the course of the years since the Reformation. In its revulsion from ecclesiasticism, the Protestant church, except a few communions such as the Lutherans and the Anglicans, attempted as far as possible to do without any definite form. But formalism and form are two quite different things. Some form or order is indispensable for the concerted action of a group of considerable size. Such form as they found to be necessary was made the simplest and barest possible. Revolting from ecclesiasticism they stressed instruction and exhortation; worship, as worship, was not cultivated.

In recent years there has been a growing appreciation in the Protestant church of the supreme value of worship and attempt has been made to recover its use. This movement, however, often spoken of as a movement to "enrich" the service, has not been fully successful. The problem has not been worked out critically enough; treatment has often been superficial. Instead of treating the matter radically, there has been much eclectic borrowing from liturgical and ritualistic services. Curiously enough, much of this borrowed material has not infrequently been taken from its native and inherently significant setting and so placed and used as to make it little more than a formal, conventional thing!

Opposed to ecclesiasticism, Protestant churches have, for the most part, extolled the idea of spontaneity in the conduct of their services. An impromptu service has been their ideal; freedom of choice has been taken as their principle and has become their tradition. But for the effective action of a group, some pre-arrangement, some preparation is requisite. Then too, mere freedom of choice is not an intelligent principle to follow. Freedom is one thing; choice is another. If it is to be successfully exercised, freedom requires knowledge, intelligence and discernment. Effective choice is dependent upon the capability of the one making it.

The adoption of freedom of choice as a leading principle and tradition seeks to preserve at least the fiction of a spontaneously inspired service. But, as a matter of fact, owing to the character and exigencies of concerted action in such a thing as public worship, "the order of service" has come to be not a really impromptu service. Most of its parts are generally prepared. Indeed, if this were not so, there would be deep resentment on the part of the worshipers. But though the several parts are carefully prepared by clergy and church musicians, they are not correlated—and there's the rub!

Separately prepared, the clerical and musical items are in

large part arranged in alternation in the service, the musical parts being used to separate the clerical. This results in a more or less chance program. Even if the clerical parts, which are naturally the more numerous, have a single theme or purpose, their consistency is disrupted by the interpolation of musical parts unrelated to them. Thus, not becoming integral items in the service, these musical parts are felt to be intrusions or mere conventions. Anthems and other choir numbers appear as interjected musical selections, while interspersed hymns not infrequently take on the character of presumably pious exercises assigned to the congregation in order to recognize and include them in the proceedings. So it comes about that the opening exercises in the order of worship are likely to have, and all too often do have, the character of a succession of miscellanies.

With how many jibes has church music been afflicted through incongruities which have appeared between itself and the sermon! Now congruities and incongruities are terms of relation and imply the presence of two parties. It is possible to regard the clerical as incongruous with the musical, or the musical as incongruous with the clerical. Religion has many phases, some of which are highly contrasted; and the minister makes choice of what shall be given place in the particular service. The musical parts selected for a service may in themselves be admirable both textually and musically and yet not be appropriate in this or that specific connection. Church musicians are often blamed for things which are not within their control.

In order to gain unity and avoid incongruities, the sermon has in many instances been selected as a centre about which everything in the service is built. This is indeed an improvement over blind chance, but it is surely not an ideal scheme. It has great defects. In the first place, such a service is entirely dominated by a single thought and mood and does not take cognizance of the fact that congregations are composed of persons having various spiritual needs and moods. In the second place, such a service confines itself unnecessarily to the personal outlook and mood of the minister; thirdly, it fails to recognize the intrinsic value which worship has in its own right; and fourthly, having an ever-changing centre about which all else must be grouped, the sermon-centred service makes constant the difficult problem of church service construction, a problem often unsatisfactorily and ineffectively handled.

Fitting the sermon, if it is not to be done superficially, requires religious insight on the part of the director of music, wide acquaintance with suitable materials, resourceful use of a well-stocked church music library, and ability in rapid preparation on the part of his choir. Unless the minister is very forehanded in his sermonizing and there are close relationships between him and the choirmaster, the latter cannot plan his work as he ought, and the congregation is likely to have hastily selected and poorly prepared music. The sermon-centred plan is all too likely to result in the selection of weak and sentimental music, inadequately prepared, the choir constantly living from hand to mouth, and half-baked bread for the congregation.

Now many of the demands which the ever-changing sermon-centred service makes are not really necessary for attaining an effective religious service. It is possible for services to be so conceived and composed as to avoid excessive requirements for either clergy or choir, and also to protect the congregation against the personal limitations—and it may be idiosyncrasies —of minister and choirmaster. They may be so constituted and conducted as also to afford the congregation opportunity and means of entering into the worship more fully and more intimately. And this may be done without reducing the influence and power of the sermon.

Between the preaching and the devotional parts of the service there should not be any conflict. Each is important. Though their functions are different, their aim is the same. Ignoring either diminishes the force and value of the service. In the past minister and choir have often been two contending parties, each very self-important, each very jealous. On the one hand, clergymen have sometimes treated both congregational and choir music as a matter of mere sufferance and concession. They have selected hymns without any apparent appropriateness, have announced them listlessly, and designated stanzas seemingly without a particle of consideration as to their meaning. They have sometimes issued instruction to have this or that in the choir's part of the service cut down or done away with, so as to give more time for their sermon. On the other hand, it must be confessed, choirs have been known to attract too much attention to themselves, to use up too much time and to monopolize the service for their own particular gratification, or, it may be in some instances, to make their own appointment seem justified to their employers by their obvious efficiency and prominence in the service.

The real source of these contentions—and the resulting ineffectiveness of music in the church service, and also of the church service itself—is a lack of appreciation of the vital character of worship. Because there is little recognition of the value and need of a really devotional element and because no adequate provision has been made for a vitally constituted and well constructed devotional service suitable for allowing music to function as it may in promoting worship, church music has tended to attract attention to itself. As a consequence the music of the church has been merely music in church and not genuine church music.

THE ABSENCE of a considerable genuine devotional element in a religious service is a serious defect. The best and noblest in man is nurtured by it. Christian worship is an informed, intelligent worship, nobly inspired and nobly inspiring. Divine worship—adoration, aspiration, communion and dedication—is the highest act of man. In a religious service worship should have its rightful place.

Though the sermon, which is naturally expository and hortatory in character, ought always to have a certain devotional tone, it is most desirable to have clear differentiation of the period of worship and that of the sermon. Their activities are so different in character and purpose, in manner and temper, as naturally to constitute two elements in the church service. The God-consciousness in the period of worship is of quite a different character from the God-consciousness in the sermonic period. They are supplementary. Each has its own contribution to make and gains by having its distinctive quality intensified and its function fully developed.

The movement to enrich the church service indicates a craving for worship. Such craving is healthful and should be satisfied. The attempts to meet it by beautifying and decorating the service in this way and that are often superficial. Neither is reversion to mediaevalism a solution of the problem. The musical past, it is true, has much to teach us, much that we should take seriously to heart, much that we should use to improve our technique in composition and absorb into our ideal, but the problems and need of the Protestant church, which we are now considering, are not to be solved and met by adoption of Roman music of the sixteenth and earlier centuries. And it is not to the improvising of special musical services that chief attention should be given, but to improving the religious character and effectiveness of the regular services of the church in both content and structure. It is the regular services which are of prime importance; they are the backbone of the church religiously. Unfortunately they have not in the past received their due meed of attention. The services of the church are wrongly conceived when congregations and choirs come out in full numbers only twice a year—on Christmas and Easter Sundays. On these festival Sundays, as we know, all the churches are crowded—in some instances there are even duplicate services and admission is "by card," while on other Sundays the attendance is small. Mere celebration is often seen to transcend worship.

THE FOURTH type of service is the free-liturgical. This is especially apt for Protestant worship. In it the priesthood of the laity may function more fully than it commonly does in the order of service. It is based upon ideals found in the order of service and develops certain of its procedures and at the same time it utilizes certain desirable principles of worship and species of devotional material found in the ritualistic-liturgical type of service. It is not, however, merely a combination of these services or a compromise, but an organic service having distinctive character and great potential value. It should replace the present faulty order of service.

Devoid, as it may be, of ritualistic implications, the liturgical principle is not incompatible with freedom. In the free-liturgical service there is freedom in the selection and use of liturgical material and ample opportunity for the use of the non-liturgical, whether extempore, prepared or selected. On the other hand, the free-liturgical service does away with the restrictions of the ritualistic-liturgical service and by avoiding constant repetitions makes possible the use of a larger body of devotional material which is equally desirable.

Familiarity with service material on the part of the worshipers is of great concern in church music. Unfamiliarity with it not only imposes an unnecessary obligation on the church musicians as regards enunciation, but it also tends to establish an attitude on the part of the worshipers which is a deterrent from the highest religious appeal through music. In those parts of the service in which music is employed the attention of the worshipers is needlessly occupied with finding out what the words are and in making out the textual substance of these sections. This, by so much, detracts from the worshipers' entering fully into their meaning and spirit; the choir parts in the service tend to become regarded objectively, questioningly as to words. The use of music in such circumstances is clearly not so inwardly expressive and spiritually moving as it otherwise might be.

Then too, unfamiliarity with the devotional literature of the church and the consequent need of perfectly clear enunciation precludes the use of some of the most effective means of musical expression. In the *Te Deum,* for instance, if, in rendering the

49

phrase "In glory everlasting," the voices enter one by one in order to gain a cumulative effect, it may be impossible to make the words stand out clearly. Yet such treatment is, expressively and musically, most effective. Not for a moment, however, do we wish to be thought to underestimate or ignore the value of good enunciation. But what virtue is there in a situation in which the congregation brings little or nothing to the service, nothing whereby its religious value may be enhanced by the aid of music? And why should the capabilities of musical art for purposes of religious expression be unnecessarily narrowed? When there is no textual basis familiar to the congregation the opportunity for music to give expressiveness is very restricted.

In stressing the textual body of the service as the basis of church music, we do not wish to appear to be placing too much reliance on and assigning too great importance to words—as words. The importance and function of words in vocal music is not a matter without considerable perplexity. There are those who extol the significance of words; and there are those who extol the power of music. The latter cite the many incongruous and inane words sometimes sung at religious services with apparent propriety, or the silly and sentimental words sometimes sung at secular gatherings and reunions with apparent exhilaration to the singers. The spirit of worship in the one case, and that of jollity in the other, may persist and even abound in the presence of incongruous words. On the other hand, as said above, there are those who extol the significance of words and set little or no store by the music, excusing or seeking to redeem poor and inappropriate music by using "sacred words." In the first of the above instances words appear to be, and have been, inconsequential, but the spirit of the occasion prevailed and overcame the deficiency; in the second, the words, through their conceptual influence, may have created a sense of religious occasion, while the music was of little or no significant influence.

This question of the intrinsic and the relative influence and power of words and music in church music is not one to be answered categorically. Both language and music are subtle means of expression. In the case of church music, expressions both in language and in music often have connotations and associations which are vitally significant and moving. And furthermore, the atmosphere of worship derived from the influence of place and occasion greatly affects the influence of music; for church music is constituted not only of words and music, but of environing and other associational influences as well. But this does not mean that words and music are not important. Both are potent aids in worship, and both should be used so as to contribute their unquestioned assistance in the advancement and elevation of worship. It is not right either to extol the words and ignore the music, or, on the other hand, to extol the music and ignore the words. Why use one leg and crutch when you have two perfectly good legs to stand on?

THAT SERMONS today are generally far more contemporaneous in their outlook and appeal than the material used in the musical portions of the devotional parts of the service is a fact which should not escape consideration. It challenges correction. Many hymns, responsive readings and texts of anthems in current use are such as cannot be approved by our clear Christian conscience. Many obsolete sixteenth-century Reformation conceptions are retained in our hymn books and anthem repertory. The devotional parts of the service, hymns as well as anthems and responses, clerical as well as musical parts, should be made as vital and contemporaneous in outlook as is possible.

The task of bringing this about is difficult. Caution should be observed in throwing anything into the discard. While many of the loftiest religious aspirations have been enshrined in forms now outmoded and in conceptions now obsolete, the discarding of all in our inheritance which does not square with our present spirit and outlook and with contemporary idiom is surely not to be advised. The highest religious culture of the past should not be discounted because it is not clothed in today's style. We are in general too prone to discredit the religious culture of former times. Modern science, it is true, has discredited much Mediaeval science; astronomy has rejected astrology, alchemy has disappeared from chemistry. But this is not properly so with culture—literary, artistic, and religious. Far from it. We do well to gather up and appropriate to our needs and development the experience of the divinely-inspired souls of the past.

While considering this matter, attention should be called to the fact that the sense of the Infinite, with its veil of the mystical which is inherent in the cosmic consciousness, tends to be repressed by the scientific mind of the present age. The scientist, like the playwright who properly enacts nothing which happens before the curtain goes up and after the curtain goes down, tends to ignore all that cannot come within his purview. But the cosmos is more than that segment of things which science can embrace. The mystical aura of experience, which must be included in the religious, finds in music, the least tangible and the most intimate of the arts, a unique means of expression.

As THE Jewish and Christian writings have been constituted into a canon of Scripture, so, for purposes of worship, there should be constituted a canon or corpus of worship, a body of liturgical material derived from Holy Scripture and from literature which has emerged from the church expressive of the deepest and most vital religious experiences and aspirations of Christians throughout the centuries. The textual substance of our services of divine worship should befit their high character. It should be of pure gold. A corpus of worship, profoundly expressive of our religious faith and life, not restricted by or subservient to any ritualistic conceptions or in any way becoming a semi-ritualistic procedure, would be of immense value and potency in vitalizing Protestant worship. Such a body of liturgical material, the intimate and personal expression of the worshiper's faith and aspirations, selected and sanctioned for purposes of worship, would be a means of greatly promoting worship. Its adoption would not interfere with the exercise of freedom in the conduct of services, for in the free-liturgical service the principle of freedom is fully maintained; in it there is freedom to select from the corpus of worship, freedom to introduce other devotional matter, Biblical or extra-Biblical, and freedom for extempore or prepared ministerial utterance.

To be an efficient means of promoting worship, a corpus of worship should be so constituted as to be truly expressive of those thoughts and conceptions which are deeply and intensely religious and possess that spiritual elevation which shall inspire those using it. It should be comprehensive and reasonably inclusive. The selection of such a body of devotional material is a task of utmost importance, one to be entrusted to those of the church at large who are most competent to undertake it. Included in this group should be some whose musical knowledge and experience enable them to perceive what is suitable for musical setting, for not all Scripture or theological material is equally suited for musical interpretation. There is devotional material which is far from suggesting song. On the other hand, to take a striking example, the *Te Deum* is much more inspiring when sung than when read—it calls for musical utterance.

To be effectual, this body of liturgical material should be made intimately and significantly familiar to those employing it as a means and medium of worship. From the standpoint of worship, the familiar is desirable: the mind dwells more exclusively on the religious import. Protestant worship should be of such a character and so constituted and conducted that each may enter into it as his supreme religious expression and aspiration and through it come into communion with the Divine, receiving therefrom spiritual confirmation, insight and strength. And from the standpoint of church music, such a body of devotional material is highly desirable. By offering a vital service substance to which music may give added expressiveness, and added impressiveness as well, it affords the best opportunity for church music to function fully. And in doing this, it tends to forestall absorption in the music merely as music, and is thus a most important means of securing genuine church music.

Education in devotional religious expression is a distinct need in the church; it is pre-eminently religious education. It may be attained by formal instruction, by memorizing or otherwise becoming intimately familiar with devotional material, by incidental elucidation in the service of the material which is being used, and best of all, by experience in worship. The latter, to be most fully attained, may however need to be supplemented and cultivated by the other means. A congregation should be liturgically equipped to function in worship.

One thing has constantly to be guarded against in services of all types of public worship, that of allowing the proceedings to become merely conventional. Maintenance of freshness and vigor is essential. With the use of liturgical material there is more or less of a tendency for the worship to become merely formal. Dull conventionality is, however, a danger that lurks not only in liturgical material; it lurks also in extempore expression. A liturgical basis of worship must constantly be kept animated and vital to those employing it. To keep it so is a duty for those entrusted with leadership in worship. They may not with impunity rest complacently on the liturgical fabric of the service, however excellent that may be. As the musician must ever keep his interpretation and rendition of music fresh and invigorating, so must the minister and church musicians keep the service, its substance and its conduct, animated and inspiring.

Active participation is the distinctive feature of Protestant worship. But participation in worship is not, as is often assumed, necessarily physical, vocally or otherwise, on the part of the worshiper. Worship is a spiritual act. True worship of God is that in which we worship Him "in spirit and in truth." Music may be an aid in doing this. But in order that music may be an integral part of the service, which genuine church music should be, the worship should be so constituted and so conducted and the music be such as to be religiously significant for all. The adoption of the liturgical principle—the use by the congregation of a service-substance intimately expressive of their aspiration, faith and religious consciousness, enhanced in expression by music appropriate in character and performance —is a reliable and valid means of attaining this end. The use of the liturgical principle, it should be repeated here, does not preclude the extempore and the individually prepared or selected.

Moreover, a religiously significant and familiar liturgy not only exercises a great influence in the service itself, but serves also to prepare the worshiper for the service by anticipating its spirit. Even a vague consciousness of this spirit tends to induce a religious frame of mind. And it should not be overlooked that a distinctly devotional spirit on the part of an assembling as well as of an assembled congregation reacts on the choir and minister, stimulating and inspiring them.

For the choir and choir-director the free-liturgical type of service has very practical advantages. By offering a large body of approved liturgical material and encouraging a sound procedure as to the general working out of the service, it relieves the director of many responsibilities which ought not to be his. The designation by the church of a corpus of worship provides him with an excellent liturgical basis for the musical parts of the service. Of this material certain parts will by natural propriety be selected for rather constant, though not necessarily invariable, use, and thus, while there is adequate leeway for variety by selection from the less frequently used parts of the corpus of worship and from other sources, the area of adjustment and special preparation by the choirmaster and choir will be reduced. By having a lessened amount for special preparation, the work of most choirs could be done better; the more variable parts could be more carefully prepared and the more or less constant parts be given adequate attention so as to be ever fresh and vital.

Another advantage is that a corpus of liturgical material

provides composers with superior texts for musical setting. Naturally, composers are not liturgists. The out-of-date character of the words of many anthems in current use and the cheaply sentimental character of others are in large measure due to the absence of such an admirable body of material as would be found in a corpus of worship. It is inevitable that the adoption of a body of liturgical material for use in the devotional parts of the service would be followed in a comparatively short time by the composition and publication of effective settings of those portions in which music is employed.

The use of worthy liturgical material set to noble music, together with the ordering of divine worship in a manner more nearly approaching its proper character, would raise the status of church music and rightly stimulate church musicians. The employment of music in its highest and most exalted function would enlist the co-operation of the best and highest minded musicians.

Furthermore, the use of the free-liturgical service employing a corpus of worship to a considerable extent would promote church unity. The surest bond of unity is not doctrine or discipline, but worship. Worship unites; it is at the heart of religion. A body of devotional material of supreme religious value, which has been made intimately familiar to all those in the same general communions of the church, is a vital means of promoting religious solidarity. Moreover—and this is of the utmost importance—through the use of the free-liturgical service, with its body of profound and inspiring devotional material, it is possible for the church to become more sincere and more adequate in expression in its services, and thereby render them more valuable to its members and more intrinsically attractive to others. And lastly, the wide use of the free-liturgical service with its familiar material constitutes a potent means of the church's holding to itself what is increasingly becoming through the trend of modern business and social life a larger and larger floating church membership.

CHAPTER VII

A FREE-LITURGICAL SERVICE

THE DISCUSSION of the service has been undertaken from the standpoint of the function of music in it and the relation between the textual basis of a service and the music which enforces and illuminates it. The conclusions arrived at are not to be regarded as necessarily committing the other parts of the service to change, except as they might be inconsistent and incongruous and not readily adjusted to this part.

The Free-liturgical service is an excellent form or type of service not only with reference to the use of church music but also as a means for otherwise enhancing worship in Protestant churches. The principles underlying it are fundamental and of wide application. As the musical, clerical and congregational sections of the service are all component parts, essentially one in purpose, it is desirable in our consideration to go beyond the realm of the musical in some instances and make suggestions as to the clerical and congregational parts as these may affect the musical parts.

The "opening exercises" of the freer orders of service have in recent years come to be constituted of a larger number of items than formerly. And because the devotional portion of the service has become diversified by the use of more numerous and generally shorter musical sections, there is need of closer and more responsive inter-relationship between parts. To be coherent and most effective, the order and substance of the modern service must in large measure be determined beforehand and in conducting the service the minister and musicians must act in close co-operation.

In the past congregations have been too much listeners and

57

not enough worshipers. They have been preached to, read to, and sung to. Sermons have been listened to as addresses, and adjudged to be good or poor; music has been listened to as music merely or as an exhibition. Worship has not been duly esteemed; its uniquely religious character has not been adequately realized. In the Roman service, the transcendent act of transubstantiation is felt to attain ultimate divine reality. In contrast, the Protestant service is criticized in that in it "nothing happens"—at least nothing comparable. And this is too often the case. This great deficiency in Protestant services is due to a lack of appreciation of the supreme value of worship, together with an absence of adequate means of attaining it. The free-liturgical service, affording vital devotional material for worship and assisting church music in achieving its proper function, provides means whereby these defects may in large measure be rectified.

RELIGIOUS WORSHIP has a fundamentally characteristic attitude and a distinct mood of its own. It has seriousness, exaltation and high purpose. But though it has a pervading basic character, it has wide variation of color. There is the bright joy of glorious revelation and spiritual realization and the sombre sadness of penitence, the consciousness of the divine majesty and that of divine compassion. The hues and colors, the lights and shades in the mood of worship are indeed manifold—all expressive aspects of its essential character.

Not only does worship have a distinct character and various colors of its own; its diversities of mood have marked correlations, as for example, the sense of exaltation with that of humility, of supplication with that of courage, of gentleness and tenderness with that of strength and vigor. In worship, moreover, there is on the one hand, inducement to reflection and introspection, and on the other, incentive to action. As the various religious moods are inherently related, by contrast and by similarity, their succession in the service should not be kaleidoscopic. A vital sequence should be sought, the succession of parts being such as to enhance their individual significance and exalt the character of the service as a whole.

SERVICES of religious worship have a certain general course. Worship is progressive; it has naturally related stages. There are in general two sequential sections in its movement which are quite different in character and mood. First, there is the period of approach, an increasing and inspiring consciousness of the Living God and the essentially spiritual basis and eternal character of our life. Then there is the period of meditation and communion.

At the beginning of the service there is renewed and fresh consciousness of the Divine. The initial period is naturally spiritually objective in character. Instinctively there is a sense of awe in coming into the Eternal Presence; a feeling of reverence comes over the worshiper. As the Soul looks up to God, there is exaltation—and humility. The second section in the period of worship is contrasted with the first. Broadly speaking, the line of demarcation will generally be found at the Scripture reading, where there is a turn from the general to the particular. Special aspects of the religious, and those which are quite personal in appeal and response belong in this second period, which is more subjective in character.

The difference in mental attitude and emotional tone of these successive periods calls for different types of liturgical and musical expression. Devotional material which is liturgical in character, such as would in large measure constitute a corpus of worship, is naturally inclined to be spiritually objective and is especially appropriate and effective in the earlier part of the service, while personally prepared materials and purely extemporaneous utterance, as well as the more highly specialized and more subjective constituents of the corpus of worship, find their place most properly in the later part of the devotional period.

The music in the two sections should correspond to their differences in character and mood. As the devotional substance of the first section is comparatively universal and impersonal in character, the music should naturally be broad, majestic, and dignified; it should have a sense of spaciousness and exaltation. In contrast with this, the music of the second section, which is of more particular reference and more meditative in character, should be more intimate in mood, quieter, and generally of smaller dimensions.

In order to bring to consideration certain features in service construction and conduct which affect church music and to provide opportunity for consideration of the appropriate treatment of the various musical items in the service, we have taken as a basis for exposition the regular morning service of a sizable non-ritualistic church in which the element of worship is definitely sought.

IN CHURCHES employing the Order of Service the first section of the period of worship is variously composed. The available items are of varied character; numerically they are far in excess of what might wisely be used in any one service. Except for a processional hymn, the Doxology, or a congregational hymn, followed by some sentences and an invocation, there is in general practice little detailed uniformity. In many instances this section is composed of too many small items; it is often overmuch broken up and is very frequently lacking in directness and effectiveness. As larger items in this part of the service, churches quite variously use responsive readings, a general confession and the creed. Some churches, however, use none of these.

It has become a common tradition in Protestant churches to begin the service, after the quiet meditation of the organ prelude, with singing a processional hymn, the Doxology, or a congregational hymn. In all these cases the initial note of the service is one of joy and dignity. The ritualistic and ritualistic-liturgical services, however, begin traditionally with penitence. Strangely enough, the hymn-processional, which has become more or less common in our churches—as distinguished from the solemn processional in ritualistic churches—originated in the Protestant Episcopal church, where it is anomalous, for there should be no choral harmonized music until after the responsive verses, "O Lord, open thou our lips; and our mouth shall show forth thy praise." In non-ritualistic churches, where the feeling for the church as a consecrated place is not strong, the processional, by giving a certain stateliness as well as warmth and elation to the beginning of the service, may have a distinctly devotional value as well as serve the utilitarian purpose of getting choir and clergy into the chancel in a formal manner. In churches where the choir is in the rear gallery or in an enclosed space behind the pulpit platform, the service is very often begun with the singing of the Doxology.

Another, though exceptional, way of beginning the liturgical portion of the service where the chancel may be entered from the side between the altar or communion table and the reading desk and pulpit is for the choir and minister to enter silently, taking their respective places in the choir stalls and at the reading desk, the organ meanwhile being played softly and finally for a moment stopping after the choir and minister have kneeled in prayer. Then the choir may impressively begin the service, as an office of worship, by quietly chanting with or without organ accompaniment the words "The Lord is in His Holy Temple; let all the earth keep silence before Him," to be followed by Scriptural sentences by the minister. The ceremonial entrance of clergy and choir may be religiously significant and effective. It may be made an act of reverence, inducing reverence.

IMMEDIATELY after the processional or Doxology there is naturally a period of Divine address or of spiritual recollection. This period is usually constituted of sentences from Holy Scriptures and an invocation, and sometimes includes a confessional prayer with ministerial declaration of forgiveness. Generally it terminates with the Lord's Prayer, said in unison. In some churches certain parts beginning the service are entirely clerical, while in others they are responsively clerical and congregational, or clerical and choral. In the latter case the several antiphonal parts should be properly balanced and related as to volume of sound, speed of utterance and general temper and spirit. Two faults are quite common in responsive exercises of the clerical-choral sort: one is that the minister uses the same tone of voice he would in preaching, and not a tone consonant with prayer; the other is that the responses by the choir are weak and sentimental and perhaps sluggish. Unless the parts in responsive exercises are correlated so as to constitute a unit, they are likely to be mechanical and become unsignificantly conventional.

In many churches this period, calling the people to worship and invoking Divine Presence, is over-elaborate, verbose, and artificial. Whether extended or very brief, this section should be impressive and devotionally moving. The material of which it is constituted should be of universal application, at once profound and intimate. While there should be considerable variety in this material, it should through use be so familiar to the congregation or made so clear and obviously pertinent as to become their own deepest personal expression.

Ideal for use in this initial period of prayer which culminates in the Lord's Prayer, to cite but one example, is the first collect in the communion service of the Anglican church: "Almighty God, unto whom all hearts are open, all desires known, and from whom no secrets are hid; cleanse the thoughts of our hearts by the inspiration of thy Holy Spirit; that we may perfectly love thee, and worthily magnify thy holy Name, through Christ our Lord, Amen."

FOLLOWING the sentences and prayer at the beginning of the service there is commonly, and quite naturally, a period of praise, transition to which is often made through the versicles: "O Lord, open thou our lips; And our mouth shall show forth thy praise," and "Praise ye the Lord; the Lord's Name be praised." Psalms then naturally have a place.

Throughout the ages the psalms have been an inspiration

in Christian worship. In the Roman and Anglican churches they have always been extensively used in prose form, Latin or English. In non-liturgical churches, however, they have generally been used in metrical form and sung to music, constituting what is termed psalmody.

Formerly in the morning and evening services of the Anglican church, the psalter was used in its entirety in monthly recitation, while in the Roman church it was used in weekly and in some instances daily recitation or reading, but not in the service of the mass. In recent times, however, there has been a rubrically allowed abbreviation and choice in the English church and a new distribution of the psalter in the Roman. Nevertheless, even with the optional use of "selections" in the English church, and a reduction and reallocation in the Roman, the psalms still constitute a very considerable and important part of devotional services in these communions.

In non-ritualistic churches the psalms were at first used in metrical form sung to psalm tunes. In the course of time, with the rise of the modern hymn and hymn tunes, metrical psalms and psalm tunes became less prominent in congregational song and in the latter part of the nineteenth century, the custom was quite commonly adopted of reading psalms, or parts of them, responsively in the formal morning service. Later, passages from the New Testament and also some from the Old were sometimes introduced into the responsive readings, which however have remained characteristically psalmic.

To be valuable in modern Christian worship, unless their recitation is taken to be merely an "act of worship," the psalms must be used discriminatingly. Though the psalter contains a body of supreme devotional material, there is, however, much in it which is contrary and even abhorrent to modern Christian thought. Many of its utterances, in fact, are sub-Christian. Moreover, many interests mentioned in the psalms were of temporary concern and many references local. These naturally are now antiquated. Yet, there is to be found in the Book of Psalms the loftiest religious expression and utterance that we possess. What is inferior in the Psalter should be discarded; but that which is sublime, eternal, and ethically as well as spiritually inspiring should be made to serve the high purpose for which it is uniquely fitted. Some psalms are such as to be used in their entirety, while others are best used in excerpts.

The Psalms were intended to be sung; they are, however, not ineffective when read responsively in the service. They are, in fact, more commonly read than sung in churches in America, even in Episcopal churches. The word psalm comes from the Greek word, $\psi\alpha\lambda\mu\delta s$, meaning a tune played on a stringed instrument. That the singing of psalms was instrumentally accompanied is evident from the mention of instruments of accompaniment: "Praise the Lord with the sound of the trumpet; praise Him with psaltery and harp. Praise him with the timbrel and dance; praise him with stringed instruments and organs." Some of the psalms contain directions for their rendition, but our understanding of the meaning of these is so vague that it is impossible to arrive at precise knowledge regarding the actual musical practice of the ancient Hebrews. The structure of the psalms, their parallelism and antiphonal character, obviously demanded a short musical phrase adaptable to varying prose lengths, which may be repeated over and over throughout the psalm. The general character of the modern chant is implicit in the poetical structure of the psalms.

Chanting is an historic form of church music which should not be discarded, as it has been by almost all non-liturgical churches. That chanting has in many instances been tedious and tiresome, perhaps alike both to chanters and to those in the pews, may have been due to an excessive amount of chanting—too many or over-long psalms "sung at one standing," as is sometimes the case in the Anglican service. It may also have been due to lack of skill and expressiveness in the chanting. Then too, many of the psalms chanted may have been of themselves unintelligible to the worshiper or foreign to modern Christian thought. A corpus of worship properly constituted would include, together with other devotional material, those parts of the Psalter which are most significant religiously and peculiarly fitted for use in the church service.

The versicles ending with "The Lord's name be praised," which often precede the Psalms, naturally lead to song. The chanting of a few great verses of the Psalms is pertinent here and does not preclude a subsequent reading of Psalms. Indeed, the successive use of singing and reading in this section of the service is desirable. The period of chanting should not be long; yet it should be long enough to give distinct character and tone to the service at this point and act as a prelude, so to speak, to the reading by minister and people. Six, eight or ten psalm verses of great significance will suffice for the chanting and from ten to twenty for the responsive reading. Together they do not take overmuch time. The chanting following the versicles gives continuity to the service, while the responsive reading provides another element in it. The two may be made to constitute a single exercise.

After the Psalms in this period of praise is a natural place for an anthem. This should be spiritually objective, in keeping with the general character of this section. It should have breadth and dignity. Naturally a somewhat extended composition, it should not, however, be an anthem which is merely strung out. If, as is usual, the responsive reading had terminated in a sung *Gloria Patri,* a well-effected instrumental transition from the *Gloria* to the anthem gives added breadth and continuity to the service.

THE SECOND section in the period of worship begins with the Scripture reading. This initiates whatever special tone the service is to have. It gives the key to parts later in the service, especially to the sermon, for which it may serve as a background. Besides the Scripture reading there are generally in this section a pastoral prayer, a musical response, an anthem, announcements—not a part of the worship—the offertory, and a hymn.

In the pastoral prayer the intimate and personal office of

the minister is clearly evidenced. In this, which has regard to his special flock, he is their embodiment and their spokesman.

The prayer is usually followed by music, a "response" on the organ or by the choir. This should not be a detached item, but should be associated with the prayer; during it the minister and the congregation should maintain the posture of prayer without change. The response by the choir may be a simple or an extended ceremonial "Amen," or it may be an added prayer, "Let the words of my mouth and the meditations of my heart be acceptable in thy sight, O Lord, my strength, and my redeemer," "Lead me, Lord, lead me in thy righteousness," "Teach me the way of thy statutes and I will keep it unto the end," or again, it may take the form of an ascription, sung quietly yet with proper expression, such as the *Sanctus*, "Holy, Holy, Holy, Lord God of Hosts, Heaven and earth are full of thy glory: Glory be to thee, O Lord Most High. Amen." The words of the response should be somewhat varied from week to week, but they should always be meaningful, pertinent and generally familiar.

An anthem may properly come in this section of the service, commonly following the response after the pastoral prayer. It should usually be rather short and meditative in character. Anthems in this part of the service may be of quite varied character, but they should in general be quiet and reflective.

It is desirable to vary the regular procedure now and then and have a comparatively short composition as the first anthem in the service and an extended one as the second, reversing the usual balance, for anthems of praise are commonly cast in larger mold than those of reflection. The second anthem may then be made an independent, self-subsistent item in the service rather than a part of its devotional flow. In this case it may have a message all its own. Occasionally making such a shift tends to dispel the sense of mechanical routine in the conduct of the service; it also gives a chance for the use of anthems of praise which are short and yet appropriate to the earlier part of the service, as well as for extended anthems of the more reflective sort which may by their character be peculiarly suited to the later, more varied and subjective section.

A hymn and the offertory constitute the remaining parts of this second section of the period of worship. At the time of the offertory, there may be a congregational hymn, a solo, organ or choral music. Anthems sung during the collection often tend to have a very pronounced musical aspect. They may, however, be such as to have devotional value as well as musical interest. Much depends upon the music used and upon the manner and spirit of its performance. Generally it is better to have the offertory precede the hymn. Both offertory and hymn are then best placed, for the offertory is more easily introduced after an anthem or a prayer with choral response than between a hymn and the sermon, and on the other hand, a hymn coming after the offertory definitely closes up the period of worship as a main section of the service. There is a sudden and desirable turn of attention—from activity in participation in congregational singing to receptivity in attending to the sermon; the congregation resume their seats and the minister, as he turns to the congregation in the sermon, stands forth impressively in his office as preacher.

THE SERVICE in Protestant churches is generally thought of as consisting of two parts—devotional exercises and the sermon. But commonly after the sermon there is a quasi-devotional period, a prayer and a hymn in continuation of the thought and mood of the sermon. The prayer and the hymn, unless it is a recessional hymn, together with the benediction, constitute an incipient third period in the service; the sermon in a way may be said to be enclosed within a body of worship. This section, which may still be held consonant with and responsive to the sermon, might desirably be made a period of dedication as the proper consummation of the service. Such a period need not extend the service unduly. In fact, by a contraction of the opening section of the service, which often seems fussed up and more or less artificial, and by strengthening it at its close, the service would in many instances be made not only more vital at both beginning and end, but also as a whole shorter. Worship should have a transforming influence. Spiritual exaltation and vision should culminate and issue in religious faith and conviction and an animating sense of moral responsibility.

An ideal prayer of dedication, which might form a permanent and central part of this period, is the prayer found in the morning and evening services of the Anglican Church:

"Almighty God, Father of all mercies, we, Thine unworthy servants, do give Thee most humble and hearty thanks for all Thy goodness and loving kindness to us, and to all men. We bless Thee for our creation, preservation, and all the blessings of this life; but above all, for Thy inestimable love in the redemption of the world by our Lord Jesus Christ; for the means of grace, and for the hope of glory. And, we beseech Thee, give us that due sense of all Thy mercies, that our hearts may be unfeignedly thankful; and that we show forth Thy praise, not only with our lips, but in our lives, by giving up ourselves to Thy service, and by walking before Thee in holiness and righteousness all our days; through Jesus Christ our Lord, to whom, with Thee and the Holy Ghost, be all honor and glory, world without end, Amen."

This prayer, recited by all as a corporate prayer, followed by the benediction pronounced by the minister, is an inspiring and proper ending for a service of divine worship. Though designated in the Anglican service as a prayer of general thanksgiving, it is equally a prayer of dedication. When used, as here suggested, it should be designated as a prayer of dedication.

As change in form of service is devotionally disturbing, a period of dedication should be introduced gradually. This may be done by the use of the prayer of dedication as a ministerial prayer before the benediction, at first occasionally and later quite regularly, acquainting the congregation with it and leading them to realize its supreme religious propriety as the culmination of the service; later, it should be preceded by a collect, and finally, joined in by the congregation, becoming a most impressive and significant corporate prayer, the consummation of the service. In order to attain its effective use, a copy of the prayer, printed on a stiff card, should be placed in the pews for the benefit of strangers and those who wish such a reminder.

Apropos of the suggestion of the use of a corporate prayer as the culmination of the service, attention should be called to the fact that there are three distinct types of prayer: first, there is the ministerial prayer, which may be either extempore or prepared; second, the corporate prayer, of which the Lord's prayer is commonly the solitary example in the services of non-liturgical churches; and third, responsive prayers, such as the versicles, which promote the devotional flow of the service. The corporate prayer, it should be noted, is a culminating type, coming naturally after ministerial or responsive prayers.

Such a brief devotional period after the sermon ensures an excellent ending of the service. It avoids an abrupt and inept termination in which the congregation, especially if standing for the hymn and benediction, awkwardly breaks ranks. Instead, the ending is impressive and deeply devotional—the prayer of dedication, a brief space for silent prayer, the benediction, a moment of reverential silence, and then quiet meditating organ music leading into an appropriate postlude. An ending of this sort is desirable from the musical as well as from the devotional point of view. It redeems the organ postlude from an ignoble plight, allowing it possibly to become religiously and musically self-respecting.

SOME MAY WISH to stress the sermon, others the element of worship—by means of a period of dedication as the culmination of the service; but whatever general plan is adopted, the ending of the service should be reverent and exalted. The universal practice of pronouncing a benediction at the close of the service is based upon a profound religious instinct. That special consciousness of the Divine Presence realized in worship is properly to be withdrawn from with the same reverence with which it is approached. The benediction, the invoking or conveying of Divine Blessing, is more than a conventional formula of dismissal.

THE FREE-LITURGICAL service, utilizing the liturgical principle and the principle of freedom of choice, is a most practical and effective type of service for Protestant worship. It provides a body of liturgical material, the most intimate and personal expression of the worshiper's faith and aspiration, selected and sanctioned for purposes of worship by the church at large, and at the same time it allows complete freedom for the use of what is individually prepared, extempore or selected from various sources. The free-liturgical service also takes cognizance of the important fact that worship is progressive, that it has sequential phases, the first spiritually objective in general character, the second relatively spiritually subjective.

Naturally the use of devotional material from a corpus of worship, which tends to be dominantly objective in character, would be much larger in the earlier section of the period of worship than in the later. In this earlier part of the service there will be a strong tendency to use with considerable frequency certain material supremely appropriate to the beginning of divine worship, which through its rather constant use will come to be a staple substance for the beginning of services.

Comprehensive in character and varied in appeal, a corpus of worship would be sufficient in amount to provide devotional material for the constitution of the earlier part of a series of services, the sections after the Scripture reading being left perfectly free and undesignated. There might be a monthly cycle of these, with special ones for such occasions as Christmas, Easter and Whitsunday. Such a series need not necessarily be used in order, for occasions may arise to make deviation desirable; but normally, the series should stand, thereby giving to the services a sustained devotional character.

A FREE LITURGICAL SERVICE

Though services of the free-liturgical type will naturally vary in substance, especially in the later section, they should have general uniformity in structure. Change of form is disturbing, while variety in substance, with its accompanying breadth and freshness of appeal, is stimulating. It is wise to have several options for the musical parts in the earlier section of the period of worship to ensure desirable scope and variety, and it is also well to have certain items as common factors, such as the Lord's Prayer, *Gloria* and versicles, to give unity to the series. A few such constant items, by giving uniformity and permanence, induce affectionate attachment and regard.

As a means of promoting worship through the use of liturgical material, a service book, large or small, is far superior to the weekly printed calendar. There is about liturgical material the sense of its being fundamental and permanent; it is not something casual, something to be fancifully varied. Moreover, the very act of reading varying devotional material from a printed leaflet each week is likely to absorb too much attention; the reader is often wondering what is coming next—what the next word, the next sentence, the next thought is to be. Now this is not the right attitude for worship. A service book, on the other hand, supplying a broad and permanent basis for worship, and not having the character of something incidental and transitory, comes to be a guide and serves as a help in one's devotions.

THE CHURCH SERVICE, its constitution and conduct, is thus seen to be a matter of very great importance in the field of church music. The musical parts should not be musical numbers interjected into the proceedings. They have their justification and find their function in giving heightened expressiveness and beauty to the religious. Though the musical factor in church music may be considered by itself, the other factors—the conceptual, the ceremonial, and the associational, as we have defined these — must be included as essential elements. These latter are derived from the service. While providing a substantial liturgical basis, the free-liturgical service

71

imposes no restriction in the exercise of freedom in the ordering of public worship. In it the priesthood of the laity is not merely an ideal and theory; it becomes a reality, and in it music readily attains its distinctive purpose in the church service.

CHAPTER VIII

SUBSERVING CHURCH MUSIC

THERE IS another side of the church music problem which has not yet been mentioned: the use of music to help in maintaining the church as an organization rather than to serve religion directly as a means and medium of worship. This use of music by the church—for instance, as attraction or as an engaging activity—may be designated as "subserving church music." Although this is not a primary use, it is nevertheless an important one, for religion finds in the church and its services its most conspicuous and definite embodiment in the world and the most effective instrument for its promotion. Now as music may serve religion through the church and its services, it is necessary in a comprehensive study of church music to consider not only the nature and operation of religion and music, but also the character and function of the church through which music seeks to serve religion.

Music may be of value in helping to sustain the church as an institution of religion, but its use for this purpose is distinctly different from and inferior to that of promoting the religious quality and vitality of the church service. Subserving church music may, however, be tributary to the latter. But on the other hand, this employment of music may be detrimental to the service, for it may cause a religiously dead spot in it or even becloud its religious character.

THE SCOPE and character of the activity of the Christian church have in the course of centuries been various. In the Middle Ages the church was the foster mother of the arts and sciences, the custodian of learning, the home of culture. She embodied

73

not only the Christian life of the time but the civilization emanating from it. In modern times the various arts and sciences, which were formerly under her protection and care, have come to their maturity and attained separate and independent life in the world. Medicine, education—except religious education—philosophy, the sciences, and, to a very large extent, philanthropy, have become secular affairs.

With us here in America the church was formerly the centre of all the higher activities of the community. It was the main source of secular culture and information, the centre of secular recreation and acquaintance. With the vast extension of the field of knowledge and the great increase of various educational facilities—the university, the college, schools, libraries and the press—the church is commonly no longer the distinctly intellectual centre. Furthermore, the church is not generally, as it once was, the social centre of the community. With the establishment of various clubs and organizations, fraternal and otherwise, in communities large and small, and with the effacing of parish social boundaries by the telephone and the automobile, the character of the church as a social centre has been insensibly and inevitably changed. Yet in rural and suburban communities and also in large cities where there is no community nucleus for the individual or family, the church may still be an important means of effecting social acquaintance and intercourse.

Likewise in the field of music, conditions have changed. Musical interests have grown and expanded so that music now has become an activity quite independent of the church; it lives its own life. So it is that the church, being no longer the intellectual, social, and musical centre of the community, naturally falls back more and more upon its prime and distinctive function, the religious. Though having still to do with all life, its contacts and its conspicuous service in the world are quite different from what they were formerly. Less a controversially theological body, less a narrowly social group, less a musical association, the church is now more entirely and more intensively a religious body having a vast and profound vital mission underlying the very life of the world.

Related to all life, religion has indeed a great task to perform. Its problems are many and perplexing. Not only have changes in theological thought and in religious and ethical concepts and objectives altered in many ways the precise character and activities of the church, but also great changes in modern social and industrial life have extensively modified the character of the life with which the church has to do and consequently have modified its function. As in the field of applied Christianity the church has in times past been the promoter and custodian of learning, literature and art, of charity, medicine and philanthropy, so in the future it will be called upon to work out fundamental problems pertaining to social welfare—material, yes, but especially those which are basically ethical and spiritual. The character of modern social life must be taken into account by the church, and church music must adapt itself to the function and work of the church. Its prime function, however, will ever be that for which it was admitted to the sanctuary: to promote worship, a worship which is humanizing and spiritualizing, exalting life.

WITHIN the church at large there are two different general conceptions regarding its precise character and its place and manner of functioning in society. On the one hand, the church may be a special institution in the community, somewhat separate from it but nonetheless spiritually permeating and animating it, the leaven in the lump; on the other hand, it may not only care for the distinctly religious life of its adherents but also to a considerable extent embrace their social life, becoming what might be designated as a "church home."

Inherent in Christianity is a certain sense of sociality—the second of the two Great Commandments is "Thou shalt love thy neighbor as thyself"; spiritual and moral fellowship is basic. But sociality is not necessarily sociability, as we ordinarily use the latter word. Whether a church is almost entirely a generating centre of the spirit—a power-house, so to speak—or a place of considerable social activity as well as of generating spiritual power is a matter which in certain ways naturally affects its employment of music. Ritualistic churches are in general characteristically of the first type, while non-ritualistic churches are not seldom of the second type. Where the social character of the church is very strong it is natural that its services should be less formal than in other churches, and its music of a somewhat warmer temper and less removed from the secular. Churches will range all the way from one extreme to the other.

A GREATER REGARD for the social side of the life of its members and the assumption of care of a larger part of it by the church are seen in the addition of the parish house to the normal equipment of the modern church. Instead of the old-time vestry used for informal religious meetings and occasional church suppers, there is now often to be found conjoined to the church edifice a large and commodious parish house with facilities not only for religious meetings, but also for dramatics, reading groups, lectures, card parties, suppers, gymnastic exercises, and basket ball. Some churches are much more extensively equipped in these ways than others.

In providing a centre for a considerable amount of the secular activity of its constituency, the parish house makes contribution to the solution of the practical problem of attaining a wholesome use of that leisure time which the development of science, machinery and modern business practice, with its accelerated speed and intensified routine, affords the larger part of our population. The healthful employment of this enlarged free area of time for social life is one of the great and urgent tasks of our day, and is more and more a matter of concern for the church. It is an aspect of social well-being which the church naturally has to assume. But just how far this task is to be undertaken and in what manner, whether directly or indirectly, it is to be most successfully handled by the church—the church at large and the individual church—is problematic. It may be done either through fostering sound social ideals and aiding in their practical attainment, or by the church itself providing means of healthful and fruitful recreation and social life within its own confines and under its own auspices. Whatever is done should be prompted by the desire of promoting the religious and moral character of social life.

THE PARISH HOUSE activities of different churches vary a great deal, in number and character. Sometimes they are disproportionately developed so that the parish house overshadows the church. Instead of being an adjunct to the church, the parish house becomes the home of a social club with ecclesiastical attachment. Gatherings and entertainments held in the parish house are in many instances much more largely attended than are the services of the church, and this not only by the general community but by the members of the church.

Frequently there are too many organizations in a church, with consequent conflicts and dissipation of energy. Instead of the organizations being strong, they are weak and inefficient. The choir is not exempt from this misfortune. Good singers are not infrequently drawn away from choir service by things less consequential.

Of the various activities in the church, none, with the exception of teaching in the church school, is so closely and deeply related to its central function as is church music. On this account it should be given its proper precedence. This may be done in various ways: by planning that as far as possible those who would be valuable as church musicians are not drawn away into other activities which would preclude choir membership; by prescribing that the time and place of rehearsal be never interfered with by any other organization; and by so constituting and conducting the service that music may attain its exalted function in it, a function second only to that of the minister. Church music should be given that consideration and support to which by virtue of its function it is unquestionably entitled.

The parish house, as an additional church building, is of great benefit to church music. By providing quarters for the various social and recreational activities of the church and effecting their segregation, the parish house is indirectly a means of promoting worship; for the church, no longer serving as a place for secular and semi-secular affairs, now comes to be associated only with religious worship and religious instruction. It becomes a sanctuary. This intensifies the sense of worship which it inspires and thereby creates a condition favorable to the attainment of genuine church music. To increase the religiously associational character of the place of worship— which can readily be done—would, in many a church, constitute a great reform, enhancing the influence of music in the church service and the power of the church itself.

Furthermore, the parish house is of benefit to church music in that it relieves the choir of the necessity of rehearsing in the church and provides favorable quarters for them. Neither the choir loft nor the chancel is a desirable place for rehearsals either from a practical or from the devotional standpoint. The parish house, on the other hand, is an ideal workroom for the choir. Here the singers may be effectively grouped for rehearsing; and here there is a piano, which is a much better instrument than the organ for use in rehearsals. Then too, as practical musical problems are to the fore in rehearsing church music, the semi-secular atmosphere of the parish house is more suited to the preparatory work of the choir than is the church. In the parish house there can properly be more freedom, musical problems of a technical sort can be better treated, and the social side of the activity can be given larger scope. Moreover, the occasional practice of secular music, quite out of the devotional vein, may readily and profitably be introduced at a choir rehearsal in the parish house. Practice in the singing of fine secular music which demands brilliance and verve is very useful in improving the technique and musical capabilities of the choir, bringing it about that their singing in the service will be more animated, vital and significant. The parish house is an excellent place for doing this.

IN RECENT YEARS there has been a movement to develop the latent musical material within our churches through the organization of various choral groups. Many churches now have not only an adult choir, but also a children's and possibly an intermediate or junior choir, these latter constituting a series of groups leading finally into the adult choir. The plan has some very desirable features. In the first place, the musical resources of the church are improved and made available for use in its services; in the second place, an excellent church activity, one appealing to musical, social, and religious interests, is created; thirdly, the employment of members of its own constituency tends to induce a more conscious sense of church solidarity; and finally, and most important of all, higher ideals of attainment in church music may be engendered through the intimate responsiveness to them on the part of those engaged in choir work; and not only this, through the members of the choir, drawn as they are from the families of the church, these ideals may come to permeate the congregation and promote the worship of the church. But for this plan to be successful, charge of things must be in the hands of a fully competent person and the plan be worked out consistently. Unfortunately, directors adequately qualified for such work are not sufficiently numerous. Provision through summer schools of church music should be made by the church at large to supply the special musical and liturgical education needed for this work. Properly treated, the cultivation of musical material within a church should lead to the improvement of its services. But though the church may seek to gain an increased musical proficiency within its constituency in order to promote and exalt worship, it is not the function of the church to engage specifically in musical education. The church should, however, see to it that its music, as music, is never of a character below that of the community or its constituency.

While there are merits in the plan of developing the musical ability within the church, there are also pitfalls. The musical resources and capabilities of a church should be used for the enhancement of its services, and not for individual or group exhibition; the church service should not be turned into an occasion for affording individuals or groups a chance for public hearing. Moreover, the choir loft or choir stalls should not be used as an exercise ground for novices. The use of home talent is commendable, but the mere fact that it is home talent does not justify the perpetration of excruciating performance or the use of unworthy music. The performances of home talent may indeed be such as to drive out some of the household of faith. Church music ought not to disregard the purpose of the church nor trespass on the rights of the congregation. We have ever to be on guard against pseudo-subserving church music.

It is a fundamental and all too common error to regard "doing something" in a service, being physically active in it, as essential to participation in it. Services are often planned so that various groups may be given place in them, the doing of this or that being for the performers their part, their participation in the service. Irrelevant and unsignificant things are often introduced to enable one or another group to have a hearing, "to take part." This is a mistake. Worship is a spiritual exercise. The service should be so conceived, so constituted, and so conducted that all, whether or not they are agents in its conduct, are equally worshipers in all its parts.

ONE OF the perplexing problems of the modern Protestant church is church attendance. The services of the church are not so largely attended by its members as they ought to be and in many instances minister and choir are unduly depended upon to hold the fort and keep things going. In these circumstances church music, in its subserving phase, is not infrequently employed chiefly as an attraction to effect church attendance.

The use of music for this purpose calls for discrimination. Pleasure is an essential feature of music—sometimes, alas, absent. But to take agreeableness and attractiveness of music as the criterion in church music is an error. Church music is capable of higher use and esteem than that of serving as a mere attraction. Some people, it is true, seem to be little responsive to religion—or, should we not rather say, to the church. But this does not justify the abandonment of principles of the right use of music applied constructively in the service of religion. Is it not rather a summons to the church for self-examination as to its services, their composition and conduct? On general principles, it is dangerous to magnify non-essentials at the expense of essentials. Church music employed as entertainment is very likely to be a detriment to the church; it is contrary to the ideals of church music.

Aside from its indirection of method and failure to employ music in its distinctively high function, the use of music in church as musical attraction has another drawback. Music outside the church has advanced to such a stage that for the church to attempt to compete with it, is as futile as it is inapt. Secular facilities for amusement have in recent times been enormously increased and improved. Competition with secular entertainment is bound to lead to failure and to loss of respect for the church. Music in the church service should bend its efforts to its distinctive end and not deploy itself in the field of entertainment, exhibition, or general display. Although behind such use of music there may be the desire to attract those who may not be approached directly, it is unfortunate and humiliating to have to come to regard church music in the semblance of a decoy. Of all places, the church should be the place where absolute sincerity is found. The church, it may be said, has a missionary character and it may need advertising; but advertising has its problems and possible attendant dangers.

Sometimes, in certain instances, the church seems to be at

its wit's end as to how to keep going and in desperation turns to sundry outside aids to ensure its continuance. Maintenance of existence is apparently sought through sensational stimulation or extraneous activities. This hectic condition is most unfavorable to the production of church music of a wholesome and healthy character. Where there should be procedure based on solid and sound principles, there is vain clutching at straws. The church may indeed be put to it to overcome the inertia in human nature, but its ambition and achievement should be something more than mere self-perpetuation. Resorting to all sorts of accessories, the church seems distrustful of its own high mission. There is no greater sign of weakness in the church than for it to depend upon secular attraction to keep up an appearance of religious vitality. All this seriously affects church music.

Unsatisfactory church attendance may be due in part to the failure of the church to meet present needs and in part to an absence of spiritual aspiration. The motives actuating church attendance are commonly various, probably more so than they should be; sometimes they may seem to be of comparatively slight religious concern. On the other hand, the central purpose of the church, its services and its music, is not always so clear and so strong as it should be either in conception or in realization. Differences—dogmatic rather than spiritual, theoretical rather than real—are unfortunately unduly stressed and dwelt upon. Moreover, one often finds a breach with the present through the retention of obsolete concepts and outworn forms of worship. In short, worship is not sufficiently dynamic; the service is not adequately conceived, and often it is not effectively conducted. The casual, if not trivial, manner in which services, at least parts of them, are sometimes conducted is a very serious fault which doubtless affects church attendance.

Then there are, as we all know, many outside detractions from church attendance—the automobile, the radio, the newspaper and others. With these the church has to contend. This is inevitably so; but contention by the church should not be carried out on secular lines, on lines in which competition by the church is futile, but rather by seeing to it that the mission of the church is impressively and exaltingly presented and its high function attained. The potency of the church service is seldom anywhere near a hundred per cent. How many of us in attending church do not feel that the service is only from sixty to seventy per cent of what it might and ought to be!

The members of the church do not in general adequately realize that a large attendance of church members is a support both to choir and minister, not as a matter of personal tribute and regard, but as a co-operative force in asserting and attaining religious values equally important to all. With respect to church music, it should be said that a larger and more regular attendance on the part of church members and a keener sense of churchmanship would be a great help to choirs and relieve the dearth of effective choir members. Church attendance is not only a duty and a responsibility, but also a privilege—essentially the highest of all privileges. That it is not so valued is an indication that there is something seriously lacking in the services or something defective in its membership.

There is, of course, a natural stimulation induced by the presence of numbers of persons; the size of a congregation does have a certain influence. But this is nevertheless a matter of secondary importance, and not a prime consideration. Its influence, it should be noted, varies with different typical groups. With the evangelical group, which conceives the church as a band of disciples, the individual element and the sense of the physical presence of others is more pronounced than with the ecclesiastical. A warmer, more individually personal tone characterizes and influences their services. With the ecclesiastical group, which conceives the church as the Body of Christ, the church embraces the individual rather than is constituted of them. Here there is a more cosmic, historic, a more universal and less individually personal tone in the sense of fellowship.

As Dean Sperry of Harvard Divinity School has expressed it: "You do not have to sit in a crowded pew, or in a group circle to have a deeply social experience of religion. You may sit all alone in a cathedral, thinking and praying in solitude, and that solitude may finally be peopled by a multitude which no man can number."

THE EMPLOYMENT of music as a means of maintaining the church as an organization and instrument of religion may be various. Its highest use is, of course, that of adding beauty and expressiveness to the services of the church, thereby increasing their religious attractiveness and their religious value. But "subserving church music" includes also secondary utilitarian phases of church music. By being in and of itself attractive and enjoyable, it may be used as an inducement to church attendance; it may also be employed as an agreeable diversifying factor in the service. But these should not be such as to cause the religious character of the service to be obscured or diminished. In seeking to sustain and animate the church as an organization of religion, church music should always be made to justify itself.

Subserving church music is an indirect use of church music. As such it is a matter difficult to assess with precision and constancy. Being on a different plane from the ecclesiastical and the evangelical, it is a use of music which may either conflict or be in alliance with them. It may contribute to attaining genuine church music; or on the other hand, it may be detrimental to its attainment, and perhaps even frustrate it. The subserving use of church music calls for discernment and the exercise of much discretion.

CHAPTER IX

OBLATIONAL CHURCH MUSIC

MENTION was made early in the first chapter of the conception of church music as decoration, sacrifice, and offering. This conception was spoken of as being partial and incomplete. Music as decoration, music as sacrifice, and music as offering were there taken to constitute a group. But although they possess certain common characteristics, whereby we may designate them collectively as "oblational church music," the constituents of this group are in some ways different. Music as decoration, for instance, has a larger aesthetic element than music as sacrifice or as offering.

In general, it may be said that decoration has much to do with the aesthetic and the externally formal, while offering and sacrifice have religious qualities which pure decoration does not have. Behind sacrifice and offering are religious traditions and theological conceptions not present in decoration pure and simple. Decoration may, indeed, have little or nothing to do with sacrifice and offering. It may, however, be related to symbolism. Most commonly under decoration pure and simple comes the making of the service beautiful and pleasant through the use of flowers, and through the use of delightful music of a certain kind. The high ritualist, however, looks upon floral decoration as being without import—it has no sufficiently definite symbolic significance, no association with sacrifice; such decoration is patently more for the gratification and satisfaction of those in attendance than as an offering to Deity. In some churches music seems to be very largely mere decoration. When such is the case the music of the church is probably regarded as "music in church," though not always necessarily of the baneful sort, for in certain circumstances church music as decoration may to some extent verge upon significant "oblational church music."

Church music as decoration often has more reference to the worshiper than thought of Him who is worshiped. This brings us to the problem as to whether church music is for "the worship and glory of Almighty God" or for "the edification of worshipers": to what extent, relatively, church music should be spiritually objective or spiritually subjective. This is a matter which should be made clearer.

In worship, be it said as a basic fact, the worshiped and the worshiper are both requisite; there must be the spiritually objective and the spiritually subjective. They are correlatives. "The spirit beareth witness that we are the Sons of God." It is a fundamental error to disregard either the objective or the subjective element in worship. Both must be present.

ANTITHESIS is sometimes made, erroneously, between church music as being for "the worship and glory of God" and for the "edification of the worshipers." The use of the word "edification" in this instance is unfortunate. Richard Hooker, author of the famous *Ecclesiastical Polity,* writes of edification as follows: "Now men are edified when either their understanding is taught somewhat whereof in such actions it behooveth all men to consider, or when their hearts are moved with any affection suitable thereto, when their minds are in any sort stirred up into that reverence, devotion, attention, and due regard which in these cases seemeth requisite." Here it is seen that edification has to do with our understanding and with our hearts. The present day connotations of "edification" have more regard to the understanding than to the emotions. They are largely, though not exclusively, instructional in character, either theologically or homiletically; our use of the word "edification" does not, as it should, stress and distinctly include reverence, aspiration, and dedication. So it is that the designation of "edification" in antithesis to "the worship and glory of

Almighty God" is inaccurate, and that the discussion of the problem is conducted on wrong lines. In place of the "edification of the worshipers" should be the words "the spiritual consciousness, aspiration, and dedication of the worshipers," for both this and "the worship and glory of God" inhere in Christian worship. The two are not incompatible; indeed, they are complementary and essential elements and phases.

Those who hold to the conception of church music as an offering not infrequently look with disdain upon any emotional feature in it. There are extremists who seem almost to deny that church music should have any effect on the worshiper. In place of the inaccurate antithesis of church music as for "the worship and glory of God" or "the edification of the worshiper," they put another inaccurate antithesis:—"church music for the worship and glory of God" or "church music to make one feel good." The designation "feeling good" is loose and unscientific. There are various ways of "feeling good"; there are qualities in feeling and emotion. The loftiest thoughts and aspirations are surcharged with emotion. It is with this emotional life of the spirit that church music has to do.

FURTHERMORE, advocates of church music as offering stress its character and performance, insisting that these be "the best" and "the most worthy." The conception underlying this is sound and wholesome. Its prevalence would indeed be most beneficial. Propriety dictates that church music should not be weak in character or slipshod in performance. Although church music may not be conceived as an offering to Deity, it nevertheless has to do with Deity. The sense that this is so should be cultivated for the promotion and exaltation of religious consciousness. But advocacy of "the best" raises many questions. What is "the best"? In the first place, in determining an answer is decision to be reached by considering the purely musical aspects of the problem, from the standpoint of composition, or of performance, or both? Secondly, is "the best" to be determined by that which is traditional in the church? Thirdly, is the designation of "the best" to be made without reference to what may be of significance to the members of the congregation? Fourthly, is "the best" that which has greatest popularity and most immediate appeal? These are questions which naturally arise. They may be answered variously. Some of those who most strenuously advocate the oblational conception of church music and the propriety of "the best" and "the most worthy" are very certain as to what such music is—Gregorian and sixteenth century polyphonic music. Now undoubtedly, some periods have produced essentially better church music than others, and some church-music traditions are greatly superior to others. Music emanating from the church is, on general principles, to be preferred to that of secular or semi-secular origin. But music belonging to a period of long ago has, along with its distinct excellencies, disadvantages arising from its archaic idiom which militate against its common use today; then too, its technical composition and its proper interpretation are matters with which the modern musician is only exceptionally familiar. Protestant worship in the twentieth century, and the music suited to it, are not identical with Roman worship of the sixteenth century; yet the achievements of the past have much to teach us today both musically and devotionally.

Valuable oblational church music is that which the congregation feels to be an offering to God. It must be the spiritual offering of the congregation, not a musical offering of the choir. Too often, particularly in non-ritualistic churches, it would appear by the character of the music, the spirit of its performance and the physical placement of the choir, that church music is intended to be an offering to the congregation rather than to God. Church music should not be something with which choir and choirmaster are chiefly concerned, an affair of theirs which is given place in the service, something that by virtue of its elaboration and showiness displays their prowess and pleases their patrons; neither should it be a convention, or something whose "sacred" character, accredited as its distinctive feature, is just a pose. To be vital, church music conceived as the impersonal offering of the church, must gather up and embody the aspirations and dedication of those constituting the church.

DIFFERENT USES of church music serve different ends and are adapted to different situations. The oblational conception of church music is distinctly at home in great cathedrals. As these magnificent structures were erected *Pro Gloria Dei,* so the music within them may properly be *Pro Gloria Dei* — oblational church music. The cathedrals were built of great size and with such magnificence not so much for the accommodation of a gathering which would fill them as to be a monument to Him in whose honor they were built. Now worship has intrinsically two phases, an objective and a subjective—that which is worshiped and adored, and the worshiper. Both objective and subjective phases are in evidence in all worship, but they are found in different proportions.

In the cathedral the spiritually objective is particularly prominent. Here oblational church music is especially appropriate. The parish church, however, is quite different in character and function. Predominantly objective worship is not equally pertinent to cathedral and to parish church. The parish church building, to be sure, should be worthy, and so should its music—a point most unfortunately often neglected—but the parish church is a place of worship, a place where men may worship, rather than primarily a building erected to the honor of God. The music of the church should accordingly be such as will aid those who assemble there for worship. The conception of church music as oblation contains a great lesson for all—the importance of having church music in itself, by its character and quality, worthy of high religious service.

OBLATIONAL church music often takes refuge beneath the aegis of Truth, Beauty, and Goodness, those great blanket terms of divine idealities. By those who extol oblational church music the element of beauty is exalted, this in support of the idea that church music should be the best and most worthy of Him to whom it is offered. The phrase "to worship God in the beauty of holiness" is by some neatly reversed into the phrase "the holiness of beauty." But is this correct? Is it not to a degree fallacious? Beauty is an abstract word and does not have precise character until it has definite content. There certainly is some beauty which is in no way associated with holiness. The identification of beauty with holiness recalls the grand finale of a high school graduation oration on music which the writer once heard, a syllogism loose and erroneous at every joint: "Music is harmony; harmony is love; and love is God," the speaker thereby attempting, at least theoretically, to declare that "Music is God." The use of the general abstract terms Truth, Goodness, and Beauty in sermons and elsewhere is sometimes open to objection as to its accuracy. They sound well and they bespeak wonderful things, but in the concrete there are various sorts of truth, goodness, and beauty. Beauty is not the central thing in church music, though it is to be sought as most appropriate and desirable.

It should be borne in mind that there are great diversities in the field of the Beautiful: the moral beauty of an act in a painful event or in a disagreeable situation is of quite a different order from the pleasurable beauty of charming symmetry or pattern or of colorful sensory appeal.

Oblational church music is closely associated with ritualism and with worship which is dominantly spiritually objective. Protestantism is not uncommonly criticized as being too subjective, as being not sufficiently spiritually objective. The recent movement to enrich the church service and make its worship more objective is an attempt to meet this criticism and correct this fault. But reversion to and adoption of Roman practice and music is not a solution for Protestants; the matter should be worked out from the Protestant centre, from Protestant devotional ideals.

OBLATIONAL CHURCH MUSIC

THE TECHNICAL musical characteristics of church music should be in accord with the devotional temperament and conceptions of those employing it as a means of worship. In the church at large there will be wide degrees of difference. The music in evangelistic and in high ritualistic services, to cite extremes, will not be identical, neither will their features be the same. The ecclesiastical type of church music will differ more widely from the secular than does the evangelical. Compared with the evangelical, the ecclesiastical is less physically exciting; its rhythms are broader, longer, more staid and more restrained. Its melodic features also are more removed from the secular. There is less superficial tunefulness, less use of sensuously cloying chromatics. In its extreme form the ecclesiastical type of church music will be ascetic, as is the extreme type of ritualistic worship. Here the spiritually objective dominates; on the other hand, in the evangelical type of service the emotionally subjective may hold undue sway.

The subjects touched upon in this chapter are matters of profound importance in church music. Although subtle, they are nevertheless fundamental. A clear vision alike of the objectives and the means of attaining them enables one to have discriminating judgment in both the theory and the practice of church music.

CHAPTER X

CONGREGATIONAL MUSIC

CONGREGATIONAL music has always been in favor, at least in theory, with Protestants. In place of the hierarchical priesthood of the Roman church, Protestants substituted the priesthood of all believers, certain functions, however, such as the performance of the ordinance of baptism and the pronouncing of the benediction, being retained for those specifically designated as the ministry. Curiously enough, in Protestant worship, founded, as it is, on the general principle of lay investiture, the personal influence and initiative of the minister became dominant. Everything, except the singing of hymns, was done by him alone. In recent times there has been an extension of the congregation's active participation in the service through a recitation of the Lord's Prayer in unison with the minister, responsive readings, and also, in some instances, through recitation of the creed by all. Notwithstanding these additions, congregational singing is still the outstanding feature of the congregation's active part in the services of Protestant churches. The Roman church, it should be noted, has of late increased its use of congregational singing; but with its conception of the nature of ecclesiastical offices, popular singing in the vernacular can inevitably be but an incidental, supplementary activity.

Congregational singing is, then, the basic form of Protestant church music. It is everywhere possible and, except among the Friends, is everywhere attempted. Even where other and very elaborate musical resources are used in the service, congregational hymns generally have a place. To plan a service without including the element of congregational song is contrary to Protestant custom; without it an important element is felt to be wanting.

CONGREGATIONAL MUSIC

Necessarily congregational music will be simple. It must be within the capabilities of the congregation, such as the entire congregation may unite in. Usually only small musical forms, such as the hymn tune, are feasible. But although the hymn tune is an elementary form of musical composition, it is nevertheless a very valuable one. It has a dignity and grandeur all its own. It is, in fact, *sui generis*. Though having very considerable limitations on its musical side, it has great potentiality on its religious side. Hymn singing, of which congregational music is almost exclusively composed, is one of the most powerful influences in the field of church music. So it is that while far from exhausting the expressive capabilities of sacred music, the hymn tune is of unique value in the domain of church music. Congregational music has its own ideals and may, in its own way, be as perfect and exalted as the more elaborate music of the choir.

That congregational music is in accord with one's theory of worship and is a comparatively simple form, does not afford substantial ground for assuming that its best use is to be attained without intelligently directed effort. It is, in fact, commonly not so effective and significant as its universal prevalence and its comparative simplicity would seem to ensure. It is frequently undertaken with such indifference and lack of spirit as to be not more than a perfunctory, conventional exercise. All too commonly congregational music is highly extolled and greatly neglected. Often it receives adequate attention from no one: the minister is too exclusively concerned with the sermon and other parts of the service which are individually his; the choir is chiefly concerned with its anthems and responses; and the congregation is musically inert and without leadership. Every now and then its shortcomings and deficiencies are here and there uncomfortably felt and become intolerable. Then some change is made: a new hymnbook is adopted; the choir, which not infrequently is looked upon as having a baneful influence on congregational music, is abolished; or a season of song-services is instituted. Instead of thorough

93

consideration of the problem and adoption of an effective procedure, subterfuge and palliatives are resorted to.

Congregational church music pertains not only to the congregation, but also to the minister and the church musicians. The minister selects the hymns, and generally though incidentally—through the association of hymn and tune in the hymnal—the tunes also; furthermore, he is the presiding leader in the service and as such in many ways affects congregational music. The organist as instrumental leader and accompanist is the constituted guide and supporter in congregational singing, while the choir serves as a vocal nucleus for the congregation. But whatever minister and church musicians may do for the promotion of congregational music, the congregation should do its part. Unfortunately it is all too prone to take little interest or trouble. Often the members of the congregation sing only when they please, and as much or as little as they please, beginning here and leaving off there without any concentration or apparent seriousness of purpose. They seem to regard hymns as introduced to afford them an opportunity to sing in the course of the service if they happen to care to do so.

THE CONGREGATION is the only musical group of serious purpose regularly attempting performance without rehearsing. The choir, composed though it is of the more musically capable ones, finds it necessary to meet for practice, but the comparatively unmusical congregation scarcely ever make any pretense at such a thing. With them things are picked up at random. It seems to be tacitly and all too readily assumed that the congregation can sing at sight anything to be found between the two covers of the hymnbook. The ineffectiveness of congregational music shows the falsity of this assumption. As compared with the choir, the congregation, besides being musically a miscellaneous assemblage, has great disadvantages in being scattered over a wide area and in not having its members disposed according to their vocal parts. Choir music, to be sure, is much more elaborate than congregational and requires much more proficiency and preparation, but even so congregational music does not receive due attention and cultivation.

The most direct way of improving congregational music is through congregational rehearsals; but these can seldom be secured. Generally the matter is not regarded as sufficiently important. One of the most commonly available ways of otherwise improving congregational music is to have a short series of sermons or talks on hymns, interesting the congregation in congregational music from the hymn side. Another is to institute from time to time a series of song services carried on in such a way as to improve the hymn singing at the regular services. But best of all are rehearsals carefully planned by minister and choirmaster. Generally these are most conveniently held in connection with services, preferably an evening service, before the service rather than after it. They may be conducted either for a few weeks each year or somewhat regularly, say, one Sunday evening a month. Now and then a well-planned and efficiently conducted rehearsal, something more than a "big sing," might be feasible at a church supper in place of a speaker.

At these rehearsals both text and music should be considered, minister and choirmaster working in conjunction. Rehearsals should be conducted with energy and enthusiasm—no superfluous words or lengthy explanations, but much well-directed, intelligent musical practice. The spirit and manner should be that of a vigorous choir rehearsal. Not long, they should begin with something fairly familiar and include things both old and new, the old being reanimated and the new becoming thoroughly learned. Such a rehearsal should be in the nature of a practice, and the service in association with which it is held should in turn have its own religious character, each fulfilling its distinctive purpose.

But even where congregational rehearsals are not to be secured, the minister and choirmaster may do much to improve congregational music. They may turn to good advantage possibilities offered by the comparative frequency of the meetings of the congregation, wisely using the power of selection which is theirs. A good selection of material and discreet repetition of it may largely redeem the situation. Frequency of repetition may be made to serve as a substitute for rehearsals. But repetition has its dangers as well as its benefits. It must be skillfully managed. Too frequent and incessant hearing of even the best music causes it to become tame and stale. Through their conduct of affairs it is possible for minister and choir director to make the words familiar, meaningful and significant, and the singing of the music confident and inspiring.

THE HYMN SOCIETY OF AMERICA, together with the American Guild of Organists, has done much for the improvement of congregational music, notably by the introduction of hymn-singing festivals in which choirs and congregations of various churches unite. The hymn-singing festival is not merely a "big sing," it is not an occasion of promiscuous hymn singing, but is planned as a service of worship. The hymns and tunes are selected and arranged with this in mind. At the beginning and at the end, there are clerical devotional parts and possibly in the course of the festival a very short address pertaining to music in worship or to the spiritual character of some of the hymns used in the service. On the musical side the festivals afford a means of introducing and making permanent and general the use of new tunes of superior quality. Some of these will be of recent composition while others are revivals of sterling tunes from earlier times. The festivals are also of value in giving greater animation and more significant regard to the best hymns and tunes in current use, some of which it is well to include in these services.

At the festival only one or two choirs are in the regular choir seats, the others being disposed in groups about the church. Obviously, in order to afford room for the members of the various congregations as well as choirs, the festivals should be held in comparatively large churches. Obviously, also, ten or a dozen hymns are not to be sung in unbroken succession!

There should be some musical variation. This may be secured and the service be enhanced by the chanting of a Psalm by the choirs in the choir seats, by an anthem with organ accompaniment at the time of the offertory, or by a simple unaccompanied anthem between two of the hymns. Descants also may be introduced with one or two of the hymns; occasionally an interesting choral or hymn-tune organ prelude, based on a choral or tune just sung, may be used to give variety in the service.

Such festivals raise the standard of congregational music both as to words and as to music. And besides concentrating attention on congregational music, they bring choir and congregation into active co-operation. The choir gives its energy wholeheartedly to the work, and thereby the singing of hymns becomes the united voice in praise and prayer of all the assembled worshipers. The enthusiasm aroused at the festival tends to be carried over into the services of the several churches participating. Being united services of the various churches of the community, these festivals create a stronger fraternal feeling, and by the united character of the undertaking they strengthen the sense of religious solidarity, which may in some instances induce a desirable union of churches of the same or allied denominations.

No CHURCH uses all the hymns and tunes in its hymnbook. Out of the three to six hundred in the hymnal, a given church may use one hundred or so different hymns and tunes. Each church, in fact, comes to have what may be called its own little hymnary, a body of hymns and tunes with which the congregation is made intimately familiar. Such a collection of sacred poetry and music should be consistently developed by minister and choirmaster. It should come to include the older standard hymns and tunes universally used by the church at large and also newer worth-while hymns and tunes. The latter should be made really familiar through repeated singing either on alternate Sundays for a short period or on several successive Sundays. A record of the use of hymns and tunes in services should be kept and be consulted so as to avoid undue repetition. Care and cultivation will create a growing regard for congregational music and induce an inspiring use.

As hymns are a part of the service, their selection should properly be in the hands of the minister, who is in charge of the service as a whole. There are, however, practical musical considerations which ought ever to have place. Selection, so far as it involves music, should be made in conference or in co-operation with the music director. As hymn and tunes are conjoined in modern hymnbooks and the selection of hymns naturally includes that of tunes, the assistance of the director may often be of great value. Presumably all the tunes in a hymnal are singable, but they are not equally so for all congregations. The director of music is more likely than the minister to know whether the tunes are feasible for the congregation and whether they are sufficiently familiar to ensure their effective use. That does not mean that the choirmaster should have full sway in congregational music. Yet his counsel is important. His attention is naturally more intently directed to the musical side of congregational music than is that of the minister; he is perhaps more sensitive and more attentive to this matter than the minister, who has many other matters in mind. The selection of congregational hymns should, nevertheless, always be in the hands of the minister.

Generally there should be three hymns in each service, two in the devotional exercises before the sermon and a third after the sermon. The first hymn should be familiar, uplifting, and invigorating, universal in character and spiritually objective, a hymn of praise and thanksgiving. The second hymn may be more reflective, quieter and religiously more subjective, more specific in character. The hymn after the sermon should be a hymn of resolve and action derived from the thought and mood of the sermon. All hymns ought to be selected with careful regard as to their context in the body of the service. As they are by nature generally more expressive than impressive in their religious character, they should be placed with particular regard to what precedes. Each of the three hymns may be given distinctive character, a character appropriate to its place in the service. Such variety and propriety will tend to avoid a sense of dull routine and give pertinency and value to congregational music.

At least one of the hymns and tunes in the service should be intimately familiar to everyone in the congregation, the first hymn always so. The hymn after the sermon is likely to be special in character and perhaps the least generally known of those used in the service. Ministers not infrequently make the mistake of calling for a hymn after the sermon which, though it reinforces the theme of the sermon, is not familiar to the congregation or is not set to a tune with which they are acquainted.

In churches having a chancel the service is generally begun with a processional hymn and ended with a recessional hymn. These are largely utilitarian in their purpose rather than strictly devotional—they serve as a means of getting the choir in and getting them out in a dignified ceremonial manner, using music to give grace and charm. The processional, moreover, gives a certain warmth and stimulus to the proceedings. The processional and recessional hymns take the place of the congregational hymn of praise in the early part of the service and of the hymn after the sermon. When, as in many churches, there is no recessional hymn, the sermon hymn is generally retained as the final hymn in the service.

Processional and recessional hymns may be treated in three distinct ways. They may be wholly choir hymns, in which case they are begun and ended by the choir in an adjoining room— the choir, so to speak, emerging from a celestial distance in the processional and returning thither in the recessional. Secondly, the processional and recessional hymns may be partly choral and partly choral-congregational, as when the congregation joins in singing with the choir on the second stanza in the processional and leaves off on the last stanza of the recessional. Frequently in this case not all stanzas are sung in the processional, but only so many as cover the movement of the choir to its destination, and in the recessional only one stanza is sung before the choir begins to move. Thirdly, the processional and recessional hymns may be entirely choral-congregational. In this case the choir is ranged in the rear of the church and in the vestibule and proceeds down the aisle, the congregation joining in the singing at the start, all the stanzas generally being sung; likewise in the recessional all the stanzas are sung, the choir leaving the chancel so as to arrive at the rear of the church at the end of the hymn. Just what treatment is to be given processional and recessional hymns in any particular church should be definitely decided on. The organist and congregation should clearly understand the intended procedure; if there is any apparent uncertainty on the part of the congregation, it should be corrected by means of explicit directions in the calendar or the printed order of service.

Hymns should be used so as to have significance and impart vitality to the service. They are not properly intermissions or interludes to break up the service, to fill up time, or to relieve monotony. Neither should they be used merely as a means of affording the members of the congregation physical relief through change of posture. They should have a worthy excuse for being and possess essential religious significance.

PLACED IN ORDER of their prominence in the popular mind, the three parties concerned with church music are as follows: church musicians, congregation, minister—the minister last. Some ministers have almost nothing to do with church music; they shun it. Some, among the laity and the clergy, regard ministers as victims in the matter of church music. They are indeed sometimes victims, but not wholly so. Seldom, if really ever, are they actually helpless. In fact, there are some things which are necessary for securing vital church music that only the minister can do.

In the selection of hymns, and incidentally of tunes, in announcing the hymns, and in their conduct and attitude during the singing ministers have important contact with congregational music. Some ministers are obviously careless and thoughtless in the selecting of hymns. Many select the hymns at the eleventh hour, sometimes just before the service begins. And often this is done in the presence of the choirmaster and choir, as if the hymns were merely a matter of routine, a convention which had eluded their attention. Careless and evidently haphazard and hasty choice of hymns and tunes, as being matters of little or no consequence, has a bad influence on the choir and on congregational music. Furthermore, a belated selection makes it impossible for the organist to look over the words of the hymn and familiarize himself or his choir with them as he should, for in the time immediately preceding the service he has, in all likelihood, many things which demand his attention and which may preclude his giving the hymns the consideration they should have both from him and from his choir.

Not only in the selection of hymns but also in the designation or lack of designation of stanzas, the minister may show slight regard for hymns and congregational singing or his high esteem. Some ministers in announcing a hymn almost invariably say: "Let us sing the first two and the last stanzas," irrespective of the character of these; others apparently pay no attention to the stanzas of a hymn, always having them all sung no matter how tedious and lacking in pertinency they may be in the particular service. A discerning selection of stanzas, occasionally and not too frequently or fussily made, tends to elevate and stimulate congregational music. But omission of stanzas should be made to enhance the propriety of the hymn and not to "save time" or merely to cut the hymn down to conventional size. Omissions ought always to be announced when the hymn is given out; never should congregational singing be interrupted by announcement during the singing of change of plans. Such action shows either absence of care in selecting of hymns or downright lack of esteem of the exercise.

Again, ministers affect church music by the manner in which

they announce the hymns and by their conduct during the singing of them. Much poor congregational music is due to the unfortunate way in which hymns are presented to the congregation and to the obviously indifferent attitude of the minister to the exercise during its progress. In his well-known book on "Preaching," Dean Brown of the Yale Divinity School aptly criticizes the conduct of the minister "who announces a hymn and then goes back to his chair and sits down while the people stand up and sing it, as if praising God were no affair of his."

Not infrequently languid and ineffective congregational music is in part due to the congregation's not rising sufficiently early. The correction of this is largely in the hands of the minister. No one else, except the choir when it is in the front of the church, can secure the timely rising of the congregation as readily as the minister. He is in general charge of conducting the service, and it is eminently his place to rise first; indeed it is unfitting for others to rise before he does. In order that the congregation may be standing and ready to sing the opening measure, he should rise with the playing over of the last line of the tune. If the hymn is announced by the minister, he should, if convenient, sit down during the playing-over of the tune so that his rising may be a signal for the congregation to rise. A good start is necessary for the attainment of animating congregational singing.

The minister also exerts an influence during the singing. Being prominently in the foreground, his every movement and his attitude affect the congregation. He should at least look on his hymnbook and give the exercise his regard, even if he does not actually sing. In not having even the appearance of engaging in or showing regard for this part of the service, the minister by his personal example detracts from it. He should lend his effort to promote every part of the service. And following the same principle, the choir should vocally unite with the congregation in its responses and readings and with minister and congregation in corporate liturgical prayer.

When hymns are announced by the minister, they should be

presented earnestly and with distinction, as if there were nothing more important at that moment than to sing that particular hymn. The occasional reading of a hymn, either in its entirety or a coherent part of it, if wisely and effectively done, gives added interest and thoughtfulness to the proceedings.

In years gone by it was the custom to read the hymn before singing it. To us now, this seems unduly formal; yet the other extreme, never to read it, can hardly be the best procedure. The former practice, several centuries ago, was born of the necessity of "lining out" the hymns, because of a scarcity of hymnbooks or other reasons. As most churches nowadays have hymnboards as well as an ample supply of hymnbooks there is really no need of announcing or of reading hymns, but even so, the occasional reading of a hymn or a portion of it before singing may afford a stimulating variety and impart added significance, concentrating attention and intensifying thought. Some hymns are so familiar that it is seldom desirable to read them; yet reading is so different from singing that even these may sometimes acquire new meaning and force by being read. It is generally the less familiar and the more specific or special hymns which are most profitably read—the less familiar ones so that they may be sung more comprehendingly and less laboriously, and the more special ones that they may become more significant and more closely related to the service in which they occur. The sermon hymn is most likely to gain in effectiveness by being read before it is sung. This is especially true if, in addition to its being unfamiliar, its language is involved or the thought-content embodied in an unusual or extended poetical manner. Many of Dr. Doddridge's hymns were specially written to be sung after his sermon, virtually as a part of its thought and feeling.

Hymns of a reflective nature are more appropriately and effectively read than those of general praise, though these latter may sometimes gain by being read. It is not well always to read the entire hymn. Sometimes the reading of only a few stanzas, the more significant ones, is best. There should be an understanding between the minister and the organist as to whether or not hymns are to be read. A simple, practical device is for the minister in announcing the hymn unobtrusively to repeat its number if he is not to read it either in part or the whole.

The ideal for congregational music is to sing from memory —in the best modern Sunday schools Scriptural passages and great hymns are memorized as being essentially desirable acquisitions. Hymns may be memorized at congregational rehearsals, if these can be had, or at mid-week meetings. A foundation for this may be laid through frequent use in the service and by illuminating comments from the minister. The singing of hymns from memory is almost as different from singing from printed words and music as the singing of a hymn is from reading it. In singing from memory there is one less intermediary than in singing from the printed page. In church music much attention, a larger amount than we ordinarily think, is commonly consumed in the act of reading. Hymns are essentially liturgical, as we use that term. Singing from memory tends to deepen and exalt worship. Memory-singing is ideal congregational music. We sing the Doxology from memory; why not such great hymns as "O God, our help in ages past," "Dear Lord and Father of mankind," "Holy, Holy, Holy! Lord God Almighty," "Love Divine, all loves excelling," and the like? If right methods were used, such a thing would be possible of attainment.

Leading and supporting congregational singing is one of the essential duties of the organist and the choir. This duty is, however, often over-charged. Too frequently the organist is expected to carry along the dead weight of a reluctant and indifferent congregation and the choir to be practically a substitute for the congregation. To have the choir do most of the singing in congregational music—unless a very large part of the congregation which is vocally capable has been withdrawn to swell the ranks of a disproportionately large chorus—is well-nigh to beg the question of "congregational singing." Congregations generally fail to contribute anything like their quota in the service. There is need of education and improvement in this matter. But congregations should not merely be admonished; proper means, liturgical and musical, should be provided and favorable conditions be created for promoting and elevating congregational worship.

Choir and congregational music are sometimes thought of as being innately opposed, as mutually exclusive, and in conflict. It is said that if the choir music of a church is good, the congregational music will be poor, and vice versa. But this is not always the case, nor should it be so. Each has its field of unique value; each should be given its proper place; each should be intelligently and carefully cultivated. It is true that some choirs may look down upon congregational music as an uninterestingly simple and inferior sort of church music; and it is also true that congregations likewise have an unworthy and inadequate conception of choir music, regarding it as a superficial attraction, an embellishment, or simply as musical display and exhibition. In the one case there is failure to appreciate the function of congregational music, and in the other that of choir music. These failures are due in large measure to an ineffective and unintelligent practice. Congregational music should be so cultivated that the choir could not look down upon it as inferior, for, as has been said, congregational music may in its way be as perfect as choir music. Both congregational and choir music should be such as to add effectiveness to the church service.

THE FIELD of hymnody is vast and varied, extending through the entire course of our religious history. Outstanding, of course, is the Psalter, the hymnbook of the Jewish church and the richest source of Christian hymnody. The Psalms have ever been extensively used in Christian liturgical worship. Hymnody —as distinguished from Psalmody, the Psalms in metrical version—has in large measure been inspired by the Psalms. Hymns from all the various epochs in our Christian era are to be found in our best hymnals. In them are Greek and Latin hymns in translations made largely by Neale in the middle of the nineteenth century, German hymns by Luther and his associates translated by Caswall, Miss Winkworth and others, as well as hymns in the vernacular by English and American authors. These latter constitute the most numerous class.

Julian in his monumental dictionary of hymnology lists over ninety thousand hymns. Of these our hymnals include from one to seven hundred. Among them are hymns from all periods. There are hymns by Clement of Alexandria in the second century; by St. Ambrose and others in the fourth century; by Bernard of Cluny and others in the twelfth century —"Jerusalem the golden," "Jesus, the very thought of Thee," "Jesus, Thou joy of loving hearts." From the sixteenth century is Luther's "A mighty Fortress is our God"; from the seventeenth century Bishop Ken's morning and evening hymns, "Awake, my soul, and with the sun," and "All praise to Thee, my God, this night," with our common Doxology, "Praise God from whom all blessings flow" as the last stanza in both hymns; and from the same century is Milton's "Let us with a gladsome mind." From the eighteenth century come Addison's, "The spacious firmament on high" and "When all Thy mercies, O my God"; Cowper's "O for a closer walk with God" and "God moves in a mysterious way"; Watts' "O God, our help in ages past," "When I survey the wondrous cross," and "Jesus shall reign where'er the sun"; and Wesley's "Love Divine, all loves excelling" and "Forth in Thy Name, O Lord, I go." From the nineteenth century we have a great number of hymns; those by Heber, Keble, Newman, Faber, Baring-Gould, and Ellerton in England, and those by Holmes, Samuel Longfellow, Hosmer and Whittier in America.

Scholars have sought to define the hymn, but we feel that this has not been done with full success. The range of hymnody is broad, inclusive of various phases of religious life and experience. There are hymns that are doctrinal—some of the earliest were such—and others that are didactic, lyrical, evangelistic, devotional. A wide range and great diversity! Hymns, moreover, may be dominantly spiritually objective or spiritually subjective. They may range from hymns of adoration, such as "Holy, Holy, Holy! Lord God Almighty," to hymns of ethical summons, such as "A charge to keep I have." Religious hymns must inevitably be both spiritually objective and spiritually subjective. In a given instance, the objective phase or the subjective phase of worship may be more prominently in the foreground, but both must ever be present: God and the Soul. In the first of the hymns just cited, God is in the foreground; in the second, God is in the background, but is nevertheless there, the Ultimate.

In the Protestant church, hymns have a place and an influence second only to the Bible. This is particularly so with the laity. Being in metre and rhyme, hymns are easily remembered; being melodically sung, they cling to the memory; appealing to the imagination by way of both mind and heart, they become a sustaining spiritual deposit. Charles Wesley very pertinently characterized hymns as constituting "a body of divinity." The great majority of people get their ideas of theology and religion very largely from hymns.

THE FULL VALUE of hymn singing is not realized until the singers feel the inspiration of the text. Despite the fact that a hymn is a simple form of liturgical expression and its language commonly though not always simple, its complete meaning is by no means always self-evident nor its full religious significance comprehended. Its value, therefore, may be enhanced by clerical elucidation. Comments as to the substance, source and expressiveness of hymns may often amplify and deepen the religious perception of those singing them. There is more need of education in hymnology than we commonly imagine, if hymns are to become what they are capable of being in divine worship. The great thoughts and intimations, the high aspirations and the sustaining faith to which they give utterance are things calling for illumination and freshening. Great words, phrases and ideas need to be revealed in their expressiveness, and also every now and then to be reinvested with their original force.

In Colonial days and in the early years of our national existence ministers were highly conscious of the duty of impressing the congregation with the importance and significance of music in the church service. Many sermons which have come down to us from the older divines attest their concern for sacred music. Nowadays we seldom hear from the pulpit anything about church music—hymns, liturgical material, anthems, tunes, and the proper character and function of church music. It is not desirable, however, to have discourses in praise of music, such as those of the olden divines with their encomiums and vaulting figures of speech. Neither is it desirable to have sensational, anecdotal or pedantic consideration of hymns, which has frequently been the sort of consideration given in more recent times. What is needed is to get at the inner substance of the hymns themselves and make vivid their spiritual content. In seeking to do this it is well to consider the field of hymnology broadly and individual hymns minutely. Acquaintance with the various great eras of hymnology gives breadth to religious outlook and perception, enriching and stabilizing faith, while consideration of individual hymns, their origin and source, their spiritual quality, their Biblical allusions and their religiously poetic expressiveness may do much to vitalize congregational music and the church service. The minister is the proper interpreter of hymns as well as of the Scriptures.

It is not sufficiently realized that a keen perception of the character and spirit of hymns is the natural and proper guide as to the manner of singing them. If the meaning of hymns were more deeply and intelligently perceived and their spirit entered into, there would be less demand for trivial brightness and thoughtless "snap and go" in congregational music—to redeem inertia. And a deeper perception of the meaning of hymns would, on the other hand, also avoid stolid, sluggish singing. With greater consideration of the words, joyous hymns would be sung jubilantly—religiously so; meditative hymns would be sung quietly, yet with movement. In congregational music, as in all other music, the singing should conform to the character of that to which it seeks to give added expression. The habit of singing all hymns in exactly the same way is to be deplored. Organists and congregations should be more alert as to the precise mood and spirit of hymns. If they were, they would find a rich variety among hymns, and there would be more animation and value in congregational singing.

CONGREGATIONAL music has to do with hymns and with tunes, but it is the tune which is of primary consideration, for hymns are of concern in the field of church music only when sung. The tune reflects and intensifies the mood of the hymn and of itself adds something distinctive. A hymn sung is very different from a hymn which is read.

As arts of expression, music and poetry are quite different. In vocal music, where they are united, there cannot always be perfect correlation; verbal and musical accents, for instance, may not always be made to coincide. Poetry is freer in certain ways. Music is more like architecture, inherently dependent upon repetition of phrase and balance of parts. The two arts cannot be equated item for item, and it is not necessary that they should be. But when combined, as they are in congregational and in choir music, they should be so related in spirit as to give enhanced significance and expression to the religious.

Dignity and seriousness are essential features of religious worship. They are two qualities which congregational tunes should possess. But although all hymn tunes should possess these fundamental qualities, there is among them as among hymns a wide variety of moods, corresponding in a general way to that wonderful diversity which there is in the religious mood. Some hymn tunes are vigorous and joyful, others meditative and tender; some are bright and cheery, while others are stern and solemn. Though all should be in accord with the general spirit of worship, each may give heightened color and moving power to the hymn with which it is used. The individual emotional character of tunes should be asserted and used so as to make distinct contribution to the service. The various phases of religious experience—its confidence, its faith, its courage and joy, its sense of intimacy and tenderness—should receive full expression.

As the hymn tune is a restricted form of musical composition, every means available should be taken to give animating variety in its use. Examination of the metrical index in hymnbooks reveals a large array of metres. Many of the differences in them are matters of small detail, but some are so pronounced as to create definite general classes that have differences of impression. The most important difference in the general structure of hymn tunes is between those which are large-patterned and those which are small-patterned. Hymns sung to tunes in double metre will naturally have half the number of stanzas they otherwise would. The greater size of such tunes, together with the smaller number of stanzas in the hymns and consequent fewer breaks between stanzas, gives to double-metred tunes quite a distinctive feeling and character. Compare, for instance, such large-patterned tunes as the *Austrian Hymn,* "Glorious things of Thee are spoken," *Aurelia,* "The Church's one foundation," and *Hyfrydol,* "Praise the Lord, ye Heavens adore Him" (used also with James Russell Lowell's "Once to every man and nation"), with small-patterned tunes, such as *Dominus Regit Me,* "The King of love my Shepherd is," *St. Anne,* "O God, our help in ages past," *Innocents, Monkland* and *St. Thomas,* each of these latter having various associations. Tunes of large dimensions give a sense of stability while those of smaller dimensions give rather a sense of activity. A discrete interspersion of tunes of varied size animates the service. When the hymns used in a service have many stanzas and are sung to tunes of the same general metrical size, they are liable to become monotonous and wearisome. One large-patterned tune, or it may be a distinctly small-patterned one, rightly placed in a service, may have a very refreshing and stimulating effect.

CONGREGATIONAL MUSIC

Then too, the tunes in our hymnbooks are cast in different time measures: in duple, triple, and compound metre, 4/4, 3/4, and 6/8. These differences are likely to affect their general mood and impression. Tunes in duple time tend to have greater dignity and more grandeur than those in triple time, while those in triple time may possibly have a more tender character. In simple music such as the hymn tune, the four-four measure allows for much more melodic and rhythmic variety than other measures. By far the largest number of tunes in our hymnbooks are in four-four metre; those in three-four come next, while those in six-eight are comparatively few.

A small but interesting class of tunes, the use of which may give a desirable diversity, is that which has stanzas terminating in a refrain or florid Alleluias. For instance, in the hymn, "For the beauty of the earth," sung to the tune of *Dix,* there is the refrain, "Lord of all, to Thee we raise This our hymn of grateful praise," and in Milton's hymn, recently mentioned, there are the recurrent lines as the last half of each stanza, "For His mercies aye endure, Ever faithful, ever sure." Notable examples of tunes having Alleluias are the Easter tune commonly called *Palestrina,* "The strife is o'er," and that taken from *Lyra Davidica,* commonly called *Worgan,* "Christ the Lord is ris'n today." Other examples which come to mind are *O Filii et Filiae,* "Ye sons and daughters," and Vaughan Williams' *Sine Nomine,* "For all Thy saints." The Welsh melody, *Gwalchmai,* arranged by J. D. Jones and used with Theodore C. Williams' hymn, "Glory be to God on high, Alleluia!" makes a happy use of interspersed Alleluias. Also, the well-known *Lasst uns Erfreuen,* sometimes used with the words, "Ye watchers and ye holy ones," has interspersed Alleluias.

The hymn tune is strophic in structure—the music for the hymn is not, as the Germans say, "durchcomponirt," composed throughout. The thought of the hymn is progressive, while the tune is repeated for successive stanzas. The tune properly intensifies the general emotional substratum of the hymn, expressing its general spirit and mood. The various stanzas

111

may, however, be sung so as to reflect their individual temper and mood. But contrasts in stanzas should be broad and general in character. They may be effected by the organist through change in registration, by the non-use and resumed use of the pedals, or by slight but expressive change in tempo or manner of playing. The fitting of the music to the changes of sentiment in the hymn should be only general and not over-nice, for congregational singing is mass singing, broad and plain.

THE TUNES in our hymnbooks, like the hymns, come from different centuries and epochs. In general, there are three distinctive historical types of tunes: first, Gregorian tunes, of which there are but a few which are practical for Protestant congregational use; second, chorales and psalm tunes; and third, hymn tunes of more recent times presenting quite a wide range of character.

Of Gregorian, or plainsong tunes, only one is commonly to be found in our hymnals, the tune, *Veni Emmanuel,* "O come, O come, Emmanuel." This is not, however, a tune of strictly ancient origin; it is made up of a number of plainsong phrases which were wrought into a tune in fairly recent times. Gregorian music, written in the old modes and sung in free rhythm, has distinctive character and flavor. *Veni Emmanuel* presents certain Gregorian features, such as the absence of the leading note in the cadence and a touch of mediaeval freedom in phrasing. A more distinctive tune of this historic order is *Adoro Te Devote,* which might be used as a choir hymn in a communion service. The atmosphere of the tune is peculiarly appropriate to this occasion. Acquaintance with plainsong idiom and style is beneficial to church musicians. Though this type of music may not, for several reasons, be feasible for general Protestant congregational use, even a small degree of familiarity with it is of great educational value.

The Protestant tunes of the Reformation period are of two sorts, chorales and psalm tunes. Both have sturdy diatonic character. They are, however, distinctly different in their structure. The chorale, which is related to the old folksong, is quite varied in form, whereas the psalm-tune, used for the singing of Psalms put into metre, is highly uniform and regular. Chorales are Lutheran, while psalm-tunes belong to Genevan and Scottish Calvinism.

A considerable number of German chorales are to be found in our best hymnals. Of these *Ein' Feste Burg*, *Nun Danket* and *The Passion Chorale* are perhaps the best known. Others frequently met with are *Innsbruck*, *Eisenbach*, *St. Theodulph*, *Decius* and *Munich*. Among them are two rather distinct types: those derived from mediaeval and traditional melodies adapted and harmonized by masterful hands, and those of contemporary Reformation composition. The former are freer and less formal in structure. In the field of the chorale Johann Crüger (1598-1662) and John Sebastian Bach (1685-1750) are among the most notable figures.

Compared with Gregorian tunes and with chorales, the psalm-tune is distinctly a rigid type. This feature is due to the restricted and regular metrical form used by the Psalm versifiers, and to the fact that the tunes are melodically syllabic. The best-known tune of this type is, of course, *Old Hundredth*, used now mostly with the Doxology, but earlier used for the metrical version of the Hundredth Psalm, "All people that on earth do dwell." At first this tune was used with the One hundred and thirty-fourth Psalm. The original form of the melody was not in notes of equal length, as has been the form currently found in our hymnbooks until recently, but as follows:

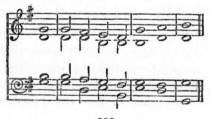

Other psalm tunes still in common use are *St. Flavian,* Day's Psalter, 1562; *Toulon,* Genevan Psalter, 1551; and *Dundee,* Scottish Psalter, 1615.

OF HYMN TUNES subsequent to the time of the Reformation there are various types. First, there is the stately diatonic type of the eighteenth century and early nineteenth century; second, the Victorian hymn tune; third, the revived folksong hymn tune; fourth, the neo-Gregorian and neo-modal; fifth, the early nineteenth century American hymn tune; and sixth, the Gospel or mission hymn tune.

A goodly number of excellent hymn tunes come from the eighteenth and early nineteenth centuries, tunes which are simple, straightforward and dignified. Their melodies employ diatonic and simple harmonic intervals, and their harmonies are those of the fundamental chords. Unlike many chorales and most psalm tunes, they do not always have one note for every syllable, but frequently have slurred and passing notes. This gives a flowing, smooth effect to the tunes. There is rhythmic freedom within a stately form. And these tunes, simple in structure and varied in their melodic character, are very sing-able. To mention a few of them, there is *Duke Street,* John Hatton (?-1793), *Wareham,* William Knapp (1698-1768), *St. Thomas,* Aaron Williams (1731-1776), *Darwall* (1731-1789), *Truro,* Psalmodia Evangelica 1789, *Melcombe,* Samuel Webbe (1740-1816), *Morning Hymn,* Barthelemon (1741-1808), and *Stuttgart,* Psalmodia Sacra 1715. The tunes of this period, with their more flowing character, call for a somewhat quicker pace than their predecessors.

In the middle of the nineteenth century a new type of hymn tune was developed in England. The leader in this was the Reverend John Bacchus Dykes, vicar of St. Oswald, Durham, who composed about three hundred tunes, of which the best known and most widely used are *Nicaea,* written for the words, "Holy, Holy, Holy! Lord God Almighty"; *Dominus Regit Me,* for the words "The King of love my shepherd is"; and *Lux*

Benigna, for "Lead, kindly Light." Other composers of this school are Barnby, Sullivan and Stainer. Compared with previous types their tunes are built on the part-song style of composition rather than on the choral. In general, they are inclined to sweetness and delicacy and tender refinement rather than to breadth, exalted dignity and sublimity. Their melodies are graceful, sometimes sensuous, and frequently depend very largely for attaining significance upon the harmonies accompanying them. The harmonies, moreover, are often of the chromatic order, at times giving the tunes a sentimental character. There is smoothness and warmth rather than strength and virility. They are, in a way, intimate in their feeling, more suited for use with subjective than with objective texts. Many of them were written for special hymns, whose moods they aim to reflect. Being cast in the part-song form, their several phrases are inherently related and balanced so that their singing is less free and more metronomic than many hymn tunes of earlier types. Their chromatic writing, together with the wide range of the several voice parts, makes many of them more suitable as choir hymns than as congregational. Some of them will doubtless become permanent valuable additions to our store of music for congregational use.

The development of the Victorian hymn tune was largely occasioned on the religious side by the Ceremonial Revival, the Tractarian or Oxford Movement, as it is variously called. On the musical side it was strongly influenced by the musical style and works of Spohr, Mendelssohn and Gounod, each of whom visited and remained for considerable periods of time in England. Each of these composers wrote for the English a number of choral works which became very popular. Spohr wrote the oratorio, *The Last Judgment;* Mendelssohn, most notably, *St. Paul* and *Elijah;* and Gounod the oratorios, *The Redemption* and *Mors et Vita.* As affecting the character of hymn tune composition in this period, it should be noted that Spohr introduced in his music a large chromatic element; that Mendelssohn introduced into England, very much to the delight of musical amateurs, the part-song, which had long existed in Germany; and that Gounod accustomed the English to that smooth and even luscious type of melody which is found in many of his masses.

In the early part of the nineteenth century there was in America a considerable cultivation of hymn tune composition, typified by Lowell Mason's *Bethany,* "Nearer, my God, to Thee," his *Hamburg,* "In the Cross of Christ I glory," and Oliver Holden's *Coronation,* "All hail the power of Jesus' name." The tunes are simple, with a tendency sometimes to plaintiveness. They are singable: their melodies are straightforward and vocal in character, and their harmonies, confined largely to the common chords in their fundamental positions and inversions used in the simplest manner, make part-singing tolerably feasible. Besides Lowell Mason and Oliver Holden, there were William B. Bradbury, John E. Gould, Thomas Hastings, Henry K. Oliver, George J. Webb, and Heinrich Zeuner. Oliver's *Federal Street,* the tune named *Webb* and sung to the hymns "The morning light is breaking," and "Stand up, stand up for Jesus," and Zeuner's *Hummel* and *Missionary Chant* are still found in almost all American hymnbooks. Lowell Mason was an important musical figure of his time. He not only greatly improved church music but also introduced music into the public schools.

In the latter quarter of the nineteenth century, the evangelistic meetings conducted by Messrs. Moody and Sankey brought into existence a new type of hymn tune, the Gospel hymn tune. Musically, it is a very inferior type, but for evangelistic purposes it proved very efficient. A mission type of tune, it found its way in certain instances into the regular services of the church, but is now used only in its proper field, where it is most effective. In England, as in America, the mission hymns constitute a distinctive class and are gathered into a special hymnbook.

Since the beginning of the twentieth century there have been two noteworthy developments in England. One is an

CONGREGATIONAL MUSIC

increased use of English, Scottish and Irish folksongs as hymn tunes. The other involves the cultivation of a type of writing which employs to a certain extent the ecclesiastical modes and also has great freedom in rhythm. The first of these movements has disclosed some effective material for use by the church, while the second, a neo-Gregorian movement, has struck out in a line which may give a more distinctive religious mood to church music.

THE IDEAL hymn tune melody is self-contained and self-subsistent, one not dependent upon an harmonic accompaniment to give it character and life. Like the best chorales and psalm-tunes, it should have meaning and vitality when sung in bare unison.

It is a moot point which is better in congregational music, part-singing or unison singing. Some hymn tunes are better adapted to be sung in unison, others in harmony, while many are equally feasible and effective either way. Though the congregation as a body is not favorably disposed in the church for part-singing, tolerably successful part-singing may, however, not be impractical. In making this possible the choir may aid greatly. Sometimes it is desirable to designate certain hymns or stanzas to be sung in unison, the others being in harmony. But to establish a uniform practice of unison or part-singing in a congregation is difficult. It would be rather hard for a church absolutely to enforce a decision, should it make one, as in all likelihood there would be some here and there in the congregation who would do as they pleased. Presumably, however, churches may be found in which there will be no such odd sticks. Anyway, congregational music is something to be joined in rather than to be listened to.

Melodies intended for unison singing should be of considerably less range than those for harmonized singing, for in unison singing the notes must be equally within the range of both alto and soprano and tenor and bass. The practical range in congregational singing is slightly more than an octave from C or

117

D up an octave and one note. This range of nine notes, interestingly, is the compass of the mediaeval or ecclesiastical vocal scales. Their staff of four lines allows for just an octave and one note. Plainsong, it will be recalled, was sung by tenors and basses in unison and without accompaniment:

Ve - ni sancte Spi - ri - tus,

In tunes of the part-song type and in others intended to be sung in harmony, the full range of the several voice parts is available; but as congregational singers are not trained singers, the extreme compass of the several parts should not be called for. All notes should be such as are comfortable, or fairly so, for all members of the congregation.

The pitch at which a tune is set in a hymnbook is not always the best for a given congregation. Not infrequently it will be found advantageous to transpose a tune down a tone, or semi-tone. It is sometimes surprising how much the singing of a congregation will thereby be improved. But care must be taken in transposing downwards against making the tune heavy and dull. In determining this matter, the size of the congregation and considerations such as the precise character and spirit of the service and the existing physical conditions should be taken into account. Occasionally the pitch of a tune should be raised.

In comparatively recent times in many of the larger churches the use of *descants* and *faux bourdons* has been introduced to add variety and heighten the effectiveness of congregational music, especially on festival occasions. Curiously enough, this newest feature in congregational music is in a way a return to a very early practice. In the earliest musical development it was the tenor, and not the soprano, who commonly had the theme. In fact, the names of the several vocal parts are derived from this early practice. The tenor is so called because it holds the theme—*teneo*, I hold; the alto part, *altus*, high, is the high part, as compared with the tenor; the soprano, *supra*, above, is above the others; and the bass, *basse*, low, is the part below the tenor. In the *faux bourdon* the congregation and the tenors of the choir sing the melody while the other three voices of the choir add a surrounding tissue by way of accompaniment. In the modern *descant* the theme, or tune, is sung in unison by all except a special group in the soprano range, who are given a free and often somewhat florid part above the theme, the organ playing the harmonies. This manner of singing—utilizing unison singing and associating with it a stimulating obligato part—may give to congregational music an animated vocal character, somewhat akin to that of elaborate choral singing. *Descants* and *faux bourdons* should be used only on certain selected stanzas, and not throughout the singing of the hymn.

In congregational singing expression should be broad and general. It should be different in different hymns, and it may be in different stanzas; but within a hymn the difference should not be overmuch. Congregational singing is a devotional act on the part of the congregation in which the words convey the thought, the music being the environing atmosphere. This atmosphere, coloring and strengthening the fundamental mood of the hymn, is important. The music may, and indeed often does, give dominating expression in congregational song. But expression cannot be concerned with individual lines, certainly not with individual words. The spirit of the hymn as a whole or of the individual stanzas should be taken as the guide. Minute marks of expression, such as have peppered the pages of certain hymnbooks and are now relegated to the limbo of dusky library shelves, are foreign to and out of keeping with congregational singing as devotional religious expression.

There is a wealth of material in our hymnbooks, both in hymns and in tunes, of which we seldom avail ourselves. Some hymnals, of course, are much richer than others. It should not be overlooked that there is progress and advancement in the field of hymnody and congregational music. Churches should not content themselves, as some do, with the use of hymnbooks which are thirty, forty or even fifty years old. There are hymnbooks which are much better than these old ones—books which have not only garnered the past but have also gathered up what is of recent and contemporary creation. Inspiration has not ceased.

No mention has been made thus far of the organist and his part in congregational music. By many he is commonly regarded as the one upon whom its success almost entirely depends. From what has been said it is clear that this is not the case, for there are other agents and many factors. The organist, however, does have a very great and important share in attaining effective congregational music. In accompanying the singing of the congregation—which he leads though seeming only to accompany—he has great responsibility for its success. As many of the ways in which he may promote congregational music are more or less technical matters they will be considered in Chapter XIV, which will have to do specifically with the part of the organist in church music.

CONCEPTIONS as to the proper character of congregational music and congregational singing are various. They are obviously quite unlike with different people. In some cases congregational singing is dull, mournful, drowsy, monotonous—as if people were doing penance; in others it is bright and even jaunty, having little dignity and apparently little seriousness. "Hearty singing" is often taken to be the ideal in congregational music. Tunes are chosen because they have a certain lilt; they are speeded up to give them gusto. But loud careless singing is not devotional. Vigor and vivacity may indeed induce physical and emotional stimulation, but this is not the all-in-all in congregational singing. Neither is loudness. Languid singing, on the other hand, is no more to be desired than mere lusty singing.

CONGREGATIONAL MUSIC

Worshipful singing should be joyful, reverent and fervent. Alleluias and hosannas should be sung jubilantly, but not with the exuberance of mere animal spirits. Religious devotional joy is not sheer excitement, nor is it the same as secular enjoyment. Congregational singing should have animation and spirit, but this spirit and animation should be of a religious character.

In its emotional character worship is distinctly reflective. Religion, always having much that is contemplative, reflective and volitional, tends by its very nature to be more intense in its inward feeling than in its outward expression. Not all hymns should be sung in a bright, sprightly way, for religion has many moods. Music should aid in their attaining inspiring expression. In hymns of praise there should be joyousness and dignity, and in hymns of prayer the sense of humility and of trust and confidence in the Divine. To blend joyousness and dignity in hymns of praise and the sense of humility and sustaining trust in hymns of prayer is a goal not always easy of attainment. Perception of the spiritual character and temper of hymns is the true guide in their interpretation in song.

CHAPTER XI

CHOIR MUSIC

CHOIR MUSIC is the highest form of church music. It does not duplicate congregational music, but furnishes another form of great value. The most highly organized and variously expressive form, it is properly the basis for the most extensive study of church music.

Choir music is distinctly representative in its nature. The choir sings in place of the congregation. Its capability, considerably beyond that of the congregation, affords an opportunity for extending the range of religious expression through music. Choir music is something more than a thing of musical beauty and interest; its function is religious—to bring the religious spirit to stronger and clearer consciousness. Through its proper use the congregation should come to realize exalted worship in which they are silent.

Worship in which music is used without vocal participation on the part of the congregation, far from being religiously passive, may be intensively active. Without absorption of attention in their own physical action, such silent worship may be more concentrated than that in which the worshiper acts as agent. Physical participation in worship may indeed be valuable in arousing and stimulating attention and interest but the efforts involved in action are liable to be more or less deterrent from full concentration. Worship is a spiritual act.

Both congregational and choir music have their besetting weaknesses. In congregational music we may be so concerned with the mechanics and act of singing—reading notes and words, uniting them, and giving them proper utterance vocally—that we are unaware of anything else. Singing in church then becomes merely an engaging exercise. And in choir music, the

122

attractiveness and enjoyment of the music may so absorb our interest that it becomes merely something musically pleasurable and charming. The practice of church music should be framed so as to avoid these shortcomings. Both the participative and the reflective are desirable in worship. Their alternation is stimulating. But that short-circuiting which is so liable to occur both in congregational and in choir music should be carefully avoided. There are means in each case of preventing it, at least in a large degree.

Intelligent direction and cultivation are requisite for the highest attainment in both congregation and choir music. Because church music, and especially choir music, requires careful cultivation is no sign, as some might aver, that it is superficial in character and artificial in method. In both choir and congregational music liturgical as well as musical matters call for consideration.

A vital textual basis is important. It is true that music apart from words may, with the aid of the various associations of place, purpose and general proceedings, be highly effective; but to put choir music in the category of purely instrumental church music does not sufficiently consider the distinctive element in vocal music—words—which in church music give expression to religious concepts and aspiration. That there may be some religious value in vocal music aside from the concepts explicitly presented in the text is not to be denied, but to rely on this possibility and give but slight regard to the distinctive feature of vocal music, is to overlook that which is deliberate and definite and cling to that which is vague and in many ways more or less uncertain in its religious influence. A really vital textual basis for the choral parts of the service is well-nigh indispensable for the fullest attainment of religious vocal music.

To be most valuable the choir parts must be placed significantly in the service. When unrelated to their environment, they tend to be merely "music in church." The pertinancy of the various musical items in the service to their context has much to do with their becoming genuine church music; they should in general grow out of the context. It is not sufficient that they be musically excellent. They should be integral parts of the service.

In general, choir music in ritualistic churches is used primarily to intensify and give color to certain liturgical material of which the service is composed, while in churches which have little or no liturgical element in their services choir music consists for the most part of anthems and solos. In other words, non-liturgical churches base their choir music chiefly on the anthem, whereas liturgical and ritualistic churches start with the musical investiture of parts of their service and only subsequently proceed to the more elaborate and special music of the anthem.

For choir music to function as genuine church music, there must be a correct conception of it. There is need of all—clergy, choir and congregation — apprehending its true function. Naturally those having charge of the conduct of services, the clergy and choirmaster, will be looked to as the ones to accomplish this. The attainment of a right attitude on the part of the congregation is best secured by a sound practice which induces and cultivates it. To establish such a practice is the task of the clergy and church musicians.

It may be well to note here that in congregationally governed churches, though the church musician is the active agent, the congregation is his employer. Herein is the reason why in general the music in such churches is not infrequently inferior as church music to that in churches which are hierarchically governed. In the latter the priest or rector is in charge of the music, and his ideals in matters pertaining to the conduct of worship are naturally expected to be superior to those of a heterogeneous congregation. He may indeed be less of an enthusiast in matters musical than a music committee composed of members selected from the laity, but he is likely to have a better conception of the purpose of church music. He may not, however, always be wise and discreet in the practical management of it.

CHOIR MUSIC

THERE ARE various types of choirs: the quartet; the soloist, by courtesy; the plain chorus; and finally the chorus with a quartet of soloists. And besides these there is also the boy choir of the Episcopal or Anglican Church.

The character and possibilities of these various types are in many ways quite dissimilar. These should be perceived and carefully regarded, and choir music be placed on an intelligent and practical basis. Too often improvement in the music of the church is sought through change from one type to another. A quartet is supplanted by a volunteer chorus, or by a single soloist, or vice versa. "A change! A change!" is the cry, and change is made with little consideration having been given to the substantial working out of the present choir body and the correction of its shortcomings, and with blithe anticipation that no difficulties are incidental to the proposed type. Some churches, happily not all, seem to be chronically afflicted with this distemper for radical changes; it is far too prevalent. Capricious alternation is futile. For one reason or another, however, it may be well to make changes now and then, but they should be made intelligently and wisely, for each type of choir has its own peculiar values and its own peculiar difficulties and each church has its own problems as to the make-up of its musical staff. The success of this or that type of choir music is also dependent upon the aims, character and method of the given church and upon general local conditions.

DURING the latter half of the nineteenth century the quartet choir was the favorite group in many churches in America. Since the beginning of the present century, however, it has not enjoyed the favor it formerly had. In some regions it has been superseded by the chorus choir. In its day and generation the quartet choir did a real service to church music in America by setting a standard of comparatively high musical excellence. But whereas the musical standard set by the quartet was beneficial, the influence of this type of choir in creating a critical

125

attitude towards the music and in inducing the secular spirit of concert performance was detrimental.

The quartet type of choir has certain obvious advantages of a practical sort. Being a small group and composed of persons who have special musical interest and capabilities, it is comparatively easily managed. As its members are usually paid for their services, they are surely to be relied upon for rehearsals and services. Furthermore, the generally long continuance of such singers in choir work is likely to increase their efficiency—yet on the other hand, choir singing sometimes becomes so set a habit that the period of one's competency is uncomfortably overstayed. Consisting as it does of four individuals, the quartet is of course subject to the acute disadvantage of having one or more of its members out of voice and of their occasionally being absent. But with such situations capable directors are always able to cope.

The quartet choir, however excellent it may be musically— and not all quartets are by any means excellent—is not ideally the most perfect organization for the attainment of genuine church music. It has some disadvantages on its devotional side and certain restrictions on its musical side.

Composed of so few persons, the individual element in the quartet is far more prominent than in a chorus. This tends to give to choir music of this type a somewhat secular character; and it also tends to induce a critically musical attitude, causing the music to be looked upon merely as music. However it is sought to overcome this—by vesting the members of the quartet and by having them sing in such wise as to merge their individual voices into an ensemble—the tendency on the part of the congregation to regard the quartet choir objectively is hard to counteract fully. The unfortunate placement of the choir in many churches behind the minister, whence they may deliver their music, as on dress parade, increases the tendency to regard the choir, especially the quartet choir, as a purely musical group and their singing as "music in church."

As the quality of tone of the individual singers in a quartet stands out prominently, it is necessary, if the quartet is to be satisfactory, that the several voices composing it should all be of a distinctly pleasing character. They should also be such as will blend and be of approximately the same strength. It is not always possible to find in a community a sufficient supply of voices which meet the requirement of good quartet singing, at least to provide quartet choirs for a large proportion of its churches.

A quartet is properly a unified musical body, a unit and not four unallied soloists. However excellent the voices may be, careful training is necessary. The several voices must be blended and balanced to make a rounded vocal ensemble. Practice in unison singing in which the voices are so blended that no individual voice is distinguishable is helpful in securing that uniformity in character and quality of tone which is desirable in ensemble singing.

The technique of quartet singing is in many ways as different from that of a chorus, as is that of a string quartet compared with that of an orchestra. In quartet singing, as in the string quartet, great attention has constantly to be paid to niceties of tone volumes and chordal balances. Differences between *pianissimo* and *piano*, *piano* and *mezzo forte*, *forte* and *fortissimo* need to be carefully gauged. The series of gradations from soft to loud is like a series of steps. In proceeding from one level to another the step should be clearly felt as a lift or a descent. To attain this, each grade must be kept at its general level throughout until the next rise or fall. By this method much variety in tone volume may be had in small-ranged variations and in extended *crescendos* and *diminuendos*. Another means of securing beauty and expressiveness in quartet singing is by bringing into due prominence the salient note or notes of chords. Beautiful resonance and fulness may thereby be secured. Too often singers shout in *forte* passages, which are sung *fortissimo*, and a disagreeable *fortissimo*, much to the annoyance of those in the pews. Still another means of securing effectiveness in quartet music—and also in extended choral compositions—is through the subtle alternation of relatively *staccato* and *legato* singing of successive phrases or sections. Expressiveness may also be obtained by varying the color of the vocal texture gained through the distribution of weight— difference in the relative strength of the vocal parts, stronger lower parts giving the sense of darkness or stability and upper parts that of brightness and animation. The intelligent and discriminating use of all such means of expression on the part of both directors and singers may raise quartet singing to a high degree of excellence and value in religious services. But though quartet music is a most refined form of church music, it should not be treated so as to be over-nice or obviously subtle.

A vast amount of music has been written for the quartet choir. Some of this is excellent, but a large part is extremely poor. Many of the means of expression peculiarly appropriate in ecclesiastical music, such as massive effects and long-sustained *forte* or extended contrapuntal passages, are not in accord with the genius of quartet music. Anthems in the heyday of the church quartet were quite frequently made up of short-breathed bits. Instead of broad dignified *crescendos* there were sudden *sforzando* climaxes, often sensational and theatrical. Structurally these anthems were likely to be flimsy and to have little continuity. Often they were little more than a string of solos for the several voices with an ensemble section at the beginning and another at the end, and possibly others interspersed here and there in the course of the composition. Many of these quartet anthems were apparently written with the intention of providing in their course a solo or duet for the several voices. But such things need not be. Their prevalence in the past should not discourage the composition of solo ensemble music for church use, provided this is adapted to the medium employed and suited to attain the function of music in religious worship. Good quartet writing as well as good quartet performance is a difficult art.

Directors of quartet choirs may sometimes enlarge their repertoire by using works written for chorus which admit of being effectively sung by an ensemble of solo voices. Some of the more extended of these may be abbreviated or only sections used.

The quartet choir and larger solo ensembles are not to be condemned *in toto* any more than the chorus choir is to be commended *in toto*. The singing in recent times of the celebrated English Singers, three men and three women, has only to be recalled to controvert the opinion that a group constituted of solo voices is inherently an inferior musical organization. The most beautiful singing and impressively religious church music the writer has ever heard was in the cathedral of the Russian Church in Paris, where the choir was composed of seven members, three women and four men. There are possibilities in choirs of this sort, as indeed also in choral music in general, which are undreamed of by many singers and directors.

THE SECOND type of non-congregational vocal church music is the solo. This is included as a type of choir music by courtesy, as a soloist is often called upon to take the place and exercise the function of a choir. Involving as it does only one person in addition to the organist, this is the simplest and most easily managed form of non-congregational music. The soloist may be permanently appointed or be a changing "guest soloist." In the matter of adaptation a single vocalist is more rapidly plastic than any choir group could be. Where only one singer is concerned, sudden adjustment to a sermon is easily made. Then too, a soloist may be less expensive than a quartet or chorus. The appealing character of the solo human voice may be religiously moving. Properly chosen and significantly sung and bound up with the rest of the service, a solo may become a valuable part of it. On account of its distinctive personal appeal, the solo type of church music is naturally more appropriate to and is more commonly employed in the evangelical type of service than in the ecclesiastical.

The solo is often likely to be productive of a mood of complacent entertainment rather than of worship and to induce a musically critical rather than a devotional attitude of mind. It is likely to be "music in church" rather than genuine church music. Although there are a small number of excellent solos admirably suited for use in divine worship, largely excerpts from oratorios and cantatas, the greater number of church solos are tame or sentimental or simply florid. Not a few are in the narrative ballad form. Many "sacred songs" are written to show off the singer; not infrequently they end with a dashing waltz-like movement and a sensational top-note climax. A scrutinizing study of the repertory available for the church soloist reveals a surprisingly small store of really first-class solos —solos which have musical and religious excellence for use in the church service. This situation may, however, be rectified in time. In general, the solo tends to be a more or less secondary and supplementary type of choir music.

There is always a danger in solo singing of the personal element being overstressed. Then too, solos may be of such a character and be used in such a way as to interrupt the service, causing it to degenerate for the time being into a concert. But this need not happen, nor is it always so. Evidence of a secularizing tendency and character in this type of church music is seen in the publication of the names of soloists in the service lists, a custom copied from the concert hall, and in the practice found in many churches of having the soloist deliberately turn to the congregation or come forward to sing his or her solo. But the propriety of this latter procedure is a matter depending upon the type of service in which it is used. The solo, whenever used, should in its devotional and musical character be appropriate to the occasion and its performance in every way be in keeping with the spirit of the service.

THE THIRD type of choir is the chorus. This is not merely an expanded quartet. Its character and temper are of quite a different devotional quality. As a musical body it has different expressional capabilities, and the details of its management are in many respects unlike those of the quartet.

The chorus choir is the type commonly desired by ministers and sometimes favored by congregations, but not so commonly desired by directors of church music, at least if such a choir is entirely volunteer. This difference of opinion on the part of the director is due not so much to musical and devotional as to managerial considerations. The director of a quartet choir is sure of its members being present at both rehearsal and service, whereas in many instances the director of a volunteer choir may have no such reliance.

Chorus choirs may be either volunteer or paid. Each is possible of being successfully conducted. Local circumstances and personal and musical conditions may be such as to make a purely volunteer chorus choir successful; but in the large majority of churches the director would greatly wish to have a small sum paid the members of the choir, or at least to a number of them, as a retaining fee to insure their presence at both rehearsals and services. With all the distractions of modern life it is generally very difficult to get constant and regular attendance, in season and out, in pleasant and in stormy weather. The payment of a small sum for the services which choir members render to the church, with deductions for absences, acts as a strong incentive to steady and prompt attendance. While affording a means of reminding them of their delinquencies through deduction for absence, it happily magnifies the responsibility of the obligation far out of proportion to the smallness of the fee. It is true that many assume and fulfil the duties of choir membership from a love of singing and from their devotion to the church; but even so, in order to fulfil this duty faithful members of the choir not infrequently have to forego various things of which the other members of the church do not have to deny themselves—a fact which congregations seldom realize.

To be effective a choir must rehearse, and those who have been at the rehearsal must be present to sing at the service. In a volunteer chorus it not infrequently happens that some come to rehearsal but do not appear at the service, or they do not attend rehearsal but turn up on Sunday at the service. The director in many churches never knows whether on Sunday morning he will have a goodly company or only a corporal's guard. This is an uncomfortable and unsatisfactory situation for the director, resulting in unfortunate treatment of the congregation. Some of this irregularity in attendance may be the director's fault through inefficient management, but generally it is not all his. The church on its part should make provision to guarantee, so far forth as possible, a worthy and inspiring service.

The shortcomings and deficiencies of a choir are many times excused on the plea that it is volunteer and that therefore a respectable standard of excellence and efficiency for its purpose is not to be required. That its music is distressing and the service is rendered vapid is not duly regarded. Such a plea is, as a matter of fact, totally unworthy of the high function of a service of divine worship.

The giving of some slight remuneration to the members of the choir has an advantage not ordinarily realized—namely, that of enabling the director to have considerable scope in admitting to membership in it. Everyone who "would like to join the choir" is not necessarily a person who would be of value to it. Some voices are the despair of the director and the ruination of the choir. Disastrous results often come from the opinion that a person with any kind of a voice may properly sing in the choir. It is sometimes very difficult for the director to decline the services of well-meaning but totally incompetent volunteers. And not a few directors find that the vocally detrimental members are the most faithful in attendance. Too many chorus choirs are, in fact, composed of a few real voices and a lot of dead wood. This state of affairs would be obviated if the director were in a position to set a value on all the voices admitted to the choir. Sometimes it is more important to keep certain voices out than to get others in.

Whether a choir is volunteer or paid is in itself not a matter of the utmost importance, but it is one which may vitally affect the attainment of its essential function. The possibility of securing an effective volunteer choir will be different in different instances; some types of community are more favorable than others.

THE CHORUS CHOIR is desirably constituted from the devotional point of view. A segment of the congregation, particularly able to promote the worship of the church through music, it accentuates the fact that in the church service all—congregation, clergy, and choir—are equally worshipers. The choir, to be sure, is a separate body set apart for the attainment of a particular function; but, though a special body, there is in a chorus choir, especially when robed and properly placed in the church, an absence of individuality in those composing it similar to that of the worshipers in the pews. This is conducive to the attainment of genuine church music.

And on the musical side the chorus is especially appropriate to religious worship. Choral tone is a composite, impersonal tone. As in the case of the congregation, where the individuality of the members is merged as they unite in common worship, so in a chorus, if rightly constituted and conducted, the individual voices are lost in the ensemble. And in addition to the merit that through the multiplication of voices and performers the vocal tone, and indeed the general character of the choir, is impersonalized, there is also the practical advantage that many voices which singly would be ineffective may when combined and merged into a unified choral tone become agreeable and constitute a dignified body of tone, ideally unindividual for use in public worship.

For a choir to be properly designated as choral there should be at least two voices on a part. Preferably, there should be three or more. Just what the number of voices on the several parts should be is a matter to be decided by consideration of the relative strength of the voices in the particular instance, for all voices are not alike in strength. A good chorus choir is one having not only good tonal substance but also effective balance of parts. With the voluntary system it is often impossible to secure this. All too often a volunteer choir is more an aggregation of voices than a unified and well-balanced chorus.

For choirs of twelve or fifteen voices harmonic music is better than contrapuntal, for unless the chorus happens to be of unusual excellence, the several individual vocal parts are not likely to possess sufficient strength and firmness to maintain their proper independence and be in right proportions. Music having simplicity and breadth, without involved part-writing, is best suited to a small-sized chorus.

A large amount of excellent harmonic choral music is available for the small chorus. In this the relation of voices and instrument may be quite various: the accompaniment may duplicate the voice parts; harmonically and rhythmically marked organ parts may be set against a unison passage for voices, or there may be antiphonal vocal and instrumental phrases; or again there may be short phrases or sections sung in unison by all the voices on a part or by a single voice; now and then short interspersed unaccompanied sections may add not only interest but expressiveness. Extended *forte* or *fortissimo* passages are generally to be avoided, since a moderate-sized chorus, unless in a small church, does not have sufficient sustaining power to maintain such passages without a straining of voices in the attempt.

THE FOURTH type of choir is the large chorus with a quartet of soloists. Such a choir permits the greatest variety of musical expressiveness and makes possible a most comprehensive repertoire. Not only may broad sustained passages be effectively sung, but contrapuntal passages, such as are uniquely pertinent in religious music, may be adequately rendered; contrasts of male and female choral sections may be had, also extended unaccompanied sections and contrasts of the full chorus with either a semi-chorus or the quartet. The presence of competent solo voices in the choir ensures the effective singing of whatever solos may occur in the music. The singers constituting the quartet, though not dominating or in any way being obtrusive, naturally serve as leaders of their several parts. Furthermore, such a chorus, merging with the congregation, stabilizes and gives a fulness and dignity to congregational singing, raising it to a high degree of effectiveness in the service.

A large chorus possesses a solid and substantial body of tone which is needed in sustained loud and in sustained soft passages, and is capable of gradation for expressive purpose. Choruses, it should be said, are generally prone to set too great store by loud singing and to indulge in singing which is indiscriminatingly loud. This may however in a large measure be impulsive rather than intentional. It is a mistake to think that the greatest impression is made by the greatest amount of sound. A choral *pianissimo* may have a subdued yet thrilling fulness of tone, like the suppression of gigantic power, often more impressive and more moving than the loud outbursts of brilliant harmonies or stirring rhythms. A certain amount of quiet music is desirable in most services; it is particularly appropriate in religious worship.

A large chorus, furthermore, has the possibility of subdivision of its several voice parts, affording musical variety and a wide range of expressiveness, and helping to avoid the monotony of constant four-part singing. The older ecclesiastical music was written for varying numbers of voice parts. In sacred music there were masses and motets, and in secular music madrigals, for five, six and more independent voices, which were persistent in the score throughout the composition. In modern church music, on the other hand, composition in four-part writing is generally taken as the basis, and increase in the number of parts is effected by divisions in the four regular voice parts. These divisions are often only incidental and temporary, the parts being divided here and there for greater fullness of chords or greater density and compactness of tonal texture. The modern Russian school of church music is especially fond of subdivisions of this sort. Chords are amplified here and there so as to become seven- eight- or nine-voiced. This music is harmonic in structure, not polyphonic like that of the early choral composers, Palestrina and Byrd, and also, though to a less extent, of Handel and Bach.

But subdivision of parts should not be indiscreetly indulged in. Music having extended passages with subdivision of parts is properly to be undertaken only by fairly large choruses. Each divided part should be sufficiently large and strong to prevent any sense of weakness, thinness, or insecurity. In brief passages these defects are not likely to be as obvious as in extended ones. For a choir successfully to use music which calls for any considerable subdivision of the voice parts, it must be possible to place absolute dependence upon having full attendance at the service.

Persistent four-part singing in organ-accompanied choral music may be avoided by a reduction as well as by an increase of voice parts. Occasional resort to two- and three-part writing is a means of gaining variety and expressiveness. It ought to be more availed of by composers, and music which is written in this less conventional manner should be more sought and chosen by choir directors. Unisons also are effective. A big choral unison with harmonically interesting and rhythmically stimulating organ accompaniment is most impressive. Moreover, in passages for a single voice part the composite tone of the chorus gives breadth and impersonal character to the music. In contrast with this, a solo voice, especially when occurring in an extended anthem, may impart a keenly human touch, arresting and appealing, similar musically to a solo violin passage in a large orchestral composition. An individual solo part in a distinctly choral work, unless it constitutes a separate number, may, however, be out of keeping with the general character of the piece, not only in quality of tone but also in quantity. Short quasi-solo passages for single vocal parts in choral compositions are often best taken by all or by a group of those of the given part; this gives tonal uniformity where diversity would be out of keeping, and especially in large church buildings ensures adequate volume, so that such sections do not appear weak and puny or fragile and insecure. Solo obligatos are occasionally met with in choral works, but care must be taken lest these become sensational. If they are rightly conceived by the composer and rightly sung by the performer they need not be cheap and tawdry, but quite the contrary.

Each of the several types of choir and choir music enumerated has its own characteristics and qualities. Which should be chosen depends upon the precise religious methods and the musical facilities of the particular church. Discussion of this and that type of church music is often prejudiced and unintelligent. No type of choir is hopeless. Choice should be made intelligently and with regard to the probabilities of the chosen form being made successful and able to promote the worship of the given church.

ROUTINE and organization are of great value in choir management, especially in the case of a large chorus. An intelligent use of pertinent routine makes for economy and efficiency. In a choir of considerable size a certain degree of formal organization is desirable. The appointment of some of their number as officers gives the members of the choir participation and responsibility in its management, and affords the director valuable assistants to whom he may delegate various duties which otherwise would devolve upon him. Every choir of considerable size should have a librarian. Such an officer relieves the director of attending to the distribution, collection and assorting of the copies of the music and thereby enables him to devote himself more fully to essential musical concerns. As a consequence of this, rehearsals move along rapidly and the service smoothly. Another valuable officer is a secretary to keep the record of attendance and send out notices when necessary. For a large choir a president, treasurer and executive committee are important officers for promoting its general management and activities, especially on the social side. The appointment of a squad leader for each part will often be found helpful in caring for the respective sections and in promoting the general *esprit de corps*.

The chorus choir of a church should be drawn from the congregation. Sometimes a director who is a music teacher or is very active in music circles enlists his pupils or friends to constitute a choir for the church which engages him, so that, although the choir may include some from the congregation, it is really the director's choir and not "the church choir" in the strict sense. In gaining recruits for the choir, the minister and music committee can be of much assistance to the director. They are in a position to know those who have good voices and would be interested in choir service. It is not always realized by the members of the church that in possessing a good singing voice they have the means of rendering valuable service to the church in the attainment of its essential purpose.

The choir is the musical guild of the church. Those who become members of it naturally do so from their interest in music and their fondness for singing. As it is through music that the choir renders its service to the church, the musical side should be duly cultivated. The members of a choir should receive musical satisfaction in their work. The fact that many of those who are engaged in choir work are attracted thereto largely by their love of music involves no valid objection to the full development of the musical phase of church music. The musical element may readily be developed without detracting from the religious; but in order to do this the musical factor must of course be rightly employed.

CHOIR MUSIC has been quite differently derived in the major branches of the church. In ritualistic and ritualistic-liturgical churches choir music was introduced to give musical investiture to various parts of the Liturgy, such as the canticles and responses; the choir in these churches was originally composed of a minor order of the clergy who were given place in the chancel, whence the designation in common parlance of this part of the church edifice as "the choir." In non-liturgical churches, on the other hand, the choir was gathered from the members of the congregation, who were assigned the so-called "singers' seats" in the rear gallery. Their purpose in the first instance was to have to do with the singing of hymns; later they came to sing an anthem of their own selection in the course of the service, and also generally a "response" after the prayer.

There are four general classes or forms of choir music: services, anthems, chants, and responses. Services, more or less elaborate musical settings of the Liturgy, normally have place only in ritualistic and ritualistic-liturgical churches. Anthems, chants and responses are used both in ritualistic and in non-ritualistic services, but they differ conspicuously in their relative prominence. In ritualistic churches responses come first, then chants, and finally anthems, whereas in non-liturgical churches the order is: anthems, responses, chants. In ritualistic services, where the Liturgy is all-important, anthems are incidental and in many instances only occasional, while in services having little liturgical material there is slight occasion for the use of chants, and responses are mostly of subordinate importance.

THE ANTHEM is the form of choir music most cultivated in non-liturgical churches. In these, the choir is commonly considered as a special musical group whose chief purpose is to provide an anthem or two for the service and probably also a response after prayer. Anthem-singing is the magnet which largely attracts to choir service and is almost indispensable in maintaining the choir as an organization.

Anthems are of two sorts, those of praise and those of prayer and meditation. The use of these in their proper places in the service—those of praise in the earlier and those of prayer and meditation in the second, the more intimate and particularized section—affords variety of inherent religious mood, and diversity of appeal, both of which are desirable. Anthems of praise generally have a certain breadth and virility, a sense of spaciousness, an exalted objectiveness. Anthems of prayer and meditation are generally much shorter, at least in the number of pages covered by the music, but, being sung more slowly, as would generally be natural, they may not take so very much less time. Constant bearing in mind of this general class distinction in anthems, together with the corresponding distinction in the two sections of the devotional exercises, creates a substantial and fundamentally varied basis for the use of anthems in the service and also invites discerning discrimination in individual pieces within each class. Where the structure of the service and the capability of the choir allow for two anthems, it is desirable that this diversity and contrast in character be utilized.

Choir music is naturally more diversified and detailed in expression than congregational music and has much greater latitude. This is true both as to words and music. Choir music has properly to do with expression of the more intimate ideal emotions. Words and thoughts in anthems may be imaginative, expressing inspiring ideals; they may be more particular and specialized in character, more poetical and highly sensitized in expression than in congregational music. It is evident that the more specialized the text and the more subtle the musical expression, the greater is the need for the congregation to understand the words.

Movement of thought in musical expression, except in certain dramatic music, is slower than in speech. The mind dwells longer and more comprehendingly on the words. And furthermore, because mood is generally more quickly established by music than by speech, music may on this account also give added force to the text. Emotion is heightened by music, yet at the same time, through the necessary formal balances in musical structure, it is regulated. This is especially true of dignified and solemn music.

Repetition of words and phrases in anthems may be a means of making choir music effective or it may be the reverse. Everything depends upon its propriety. If the repetition is occasioned merely by the formal structure of the music, it is faulty; but if repetition of words and phrases gives heightened effectiveness to the text, it is a potent means of attaining effective church music. In congregational music repetition of words and phrases is rather exceptional; in choir music, where there is greater freedom, it is a means of gaining oratorical emphasis as well as architectural impressiveness and beauty. But repetition must be significant, and not mechanical. The exigencies of musical form should not override the text.

Many anthems are tediously long. Constructed on a conventional, artificial pattern, they are unduly spun out by unsignificant repetitions. As a consequence the congregation feels that it has to "sit through an anthem." Ideally, anthems should not be extended beyond the full expression of the devotional mood of their words, nor beyond the inherent implications of their musical material. A short anthem, if well selected, well performed, and well placed in the service, is often very effective. Indeed, it is surprising how sufficient and adequate comparatively short anthems may be, if they are of the right sort and are pertinently placed. One comparatively large anthem, however, if worthy and well sung, is desirable in each service.

Both words and music ought to be excellent. Unfortunately they are not always well mated. All too often one finds good words with poor music, and contrariwise, good music with poor words. Frequently the director in his search for new music has either to compromise or to go without making addition to his store, at least, for the time being.

Many choirmasters are inert and unenterprising, using the same anthems year after year, while others are wont to introduce an immoderate amount of new music. This latter habit is often occasioned by a low level of contentment, or by the director's lack of ability to perfect that already at hand. Not infrequently "new music" is introduced with the view of stimulating the choir, keeping it interested by creating an impression of progress. But the lure of "new music" has its pitfalls. Notes may indeed be new, but there may be nothing new in the music. All too often there is simply one mediocrity after another: poor music and poor performance. Learning new notes may keep the choir active, but it is the activity of the treadmill, resulting in dull and lifeless routine.

The repertory of a choir should grow. When it does not, the choir stagnates. But the growth should not be merely in bulk; it should be an enrichment. Much of the music chosen by directors who introduce a very large amount of new music is more than likely to be ephemeral in character. Not being capable of effective repetition, the greater part of the effort put upon its preparation vanishes with its first performance. Anthems ought always to be worthy of the time and trouble expended upon them. Music which does not bear repetition to a reasonable extent is unduly expensive of effort. Furthermore, the judicious repetition of significant choir music is a potent means of improving church music in general and of securing its highest attainment both on the part of the choir and on the part of the congregation. Worthy music wears well; its expressiveness increases and its impressiveness deepens.

WHILE choir music is on a plane allowing for far more subtlety and refinement in expression than congregational music, and also more variety, on this plane there should always be propriety and excellence. That choir music may be more elaborate and more varied than congregational music does not give it unlimited freedom nor release it from the restrictions of sacred music, those incidental to the attainment of its function. Overelaboration is a common fault. Many a choir becomes tantalizingly incompetent through attempting to sing anthems which in one way and another are too difficult for them. Striving for more than the means allow, ambition o'erleaps itself. Though it is desirable that singers who are more or less accomplished should, at least for a part of the time, be given music which is up to their capabilities, care must be taken not to exceed this. To keep within bounds and yet have these bounds as extensive as possible—for choir music is an advanced form of church music—is one of the tasks of the director.

And the choir music of a church should not only be within the capabilities of the choir, it should also be within the comprehension of the congregation. It is so easy for choirs and directors to fall into the habit of selecting anthems which are interesting to themselves that frequently the congregation is not given proper consideration. The musical comprehension and responsiveness of the congregation should be taken into account; so also should the church-music tradition of the given church. But these should not be unduly acceded to or slavishly followed. Choir music should be worship-music; ideally, it should be in the language and in an idiom suited to worship and to the comprehension of the worshiper. Very often, it should be said, an incessant introduction of new music, as well as an excessive amount of choir music in the service, causes annoyance to the congregation and detracts from the value of the service.

Anthems which are complicated and involved are likely to be ineffective for congregations; ornate ones are apt to be inappropriate for use in religious worship. It is not necessarily the most difficult music which is the best or the most interesting. In many instances anthems, especially those which are comparatively elaborate, are in fact over-difficult: not having been worked out consistently as compositions, they are difficult to learn, and not having been written well for the voice, they are difficult to sing. Inferior music is sometimes harder to sing than that which is really excellent, and it is less likely in the long run to be edifying for the congregation.

Fairly simple anthem music is generally best for church use. This does not mean that it should be tame, insipid and characterless. In fact, it should be just the opposite. Some of the most sublime music ever written is simplicity itself. Music of simple structure but of high musical and devotional character must, however, be sung well. Such music makes ample requisition on the performer as interpreter, and is likely to be nearer the heart and mind of the worshiper than is music of great elaboration.

Elaborate anthems, if adequately performed, may have a profound influence in disposing to worship. They are, however, likely to be quite impossible of satisfactory performance and effective use in any but a comparatively few churches. Few choirs are vocally capable and adequately trained to ensure an impressive and moving performance of very elaborate music. In many of these compositions the organ part is so free and so interrelated with the vocal parts that the organ of the church may not be sufficiently resourceful or the organist capable in his use of it to meet the requirements of the music, to say nothing of the ability of the choir to maintain itself as it should. Every now and then it is well, in order to stimulate the interest and activity of a choir, to introduce anthems which are somewhat above the degree of elaboration and level of difficulty ordinarily used; but these should be suited to the capabilities of the choir and their proper performance should be guaranteed responses are of two kinds: first, the choir response to prayer; and second, the choral-ministerial versicles, "O Lord, open thou our lips: And our mouth shall show forth thy praise," etc., and through adequate preparation.

So MUCH for anthem music; now as to responses and chanting. In churches employing the order of service form of worship those beginning, "The Lord be with you; And with thy spirit."

First as to what is called the "response to prayer." Originally, music after the long or pastoral prayer consisted of a few chords on the organ, as an addition of a ceremonial character. But as time went on and there came to be more choir music in the service the response became choral. The words in the response to prayer should be of deep religious significance—a ceremonial Amen, a brief verse of prayer, or an ascription. Frequently the response is too much detached from the prayer: there is a long interval consumed in the choir's "getting the pitch"—presumably unobtrusively, yet actually very obviously—from a faint, far-away *aeoline*. A *dulciana* with its firmer tone is often much better, the choir coming in without a wait. Then again, the response to prayer should not be too much a hushed affair. It should of course be quiet, for prayer is quiet, and naturally also its volume of tone should be somewhat less than that of the minister, but a response after prayer ought not to be something weak and sentimental. It should have dignity and significance.

In versicles the ministerial and choral parts should be balanced. They should be integratingly complementary, the speaking and the singing co-ordinated both as to general volume of tone and as to pace, and the parts expressively and responsively spaced. All this requires active co-operation between minister and director. When not correlated the versicles become mere formalities. Choirs, unhappily, often make a languishing ritard and drag out their part as if reluctant to let go.

CHANTING, unfortunately, is little used in non-liturgical churches —no doubt because of the slight amount of strictly liturgical material in the substance of their services. It is a distinctive and valuable form of church music. For one thing, it is exclusively associated with religious worship; nowhere else is it used. Moreover, as the chant is a musical form or framework in which the music is held in subordination to the words and does not make the independent artistic impression which other music generally does, and as the words are of paramount consideration, it tends to secure genuine church music rather than "music in church." Then too, besides having intrinsic virtues, the chant is also a means of securing significant variety in the service.

The chant, as a musical form, is inherently an elastic composition intended to be adapted to an ever-varying psalm verse. Unfortunately, there is a tendency to treat it not according to its genius but in a rather staid and metrical fashion, as if it were similar to a hymn tune. Chanting is characteristically flexible music conforming to the rhythm and phrasing of the words. To secure expressive free speech rhythm in chanting is not easy. For a group to attain it the verses of the psalm should first be patterned by the director and then read by director and singers until there is unanimity in the reading; then they should be monotoned in this speech rhythm but in the somewhat slower speed of chanting, and finally sung to the chosen chant. As the verses are of varied lengths and their structure and stress not regular and uniform, chanting should be worked out largely verse by verse. To secure good chanting the singers should know the chant by heart—it is always a simple composure, and they should be so familiar with the words, together with their pointing, as to sing practically from memory. Then there will be freedom and expressiveness.

Being musical speech, the pace in chanting should not be too quick or the volume of tone excessive. These are two common faults. The feeling of racing or that the tone is forced is to be avoided. There should be a steady, even flow. Expression should be obtained through phrasing and slight variation of tempo fitting the emotional character of the text and through the proper mental grouping of the words. For the most part, chanting should be *mezzo forte* with varying volume of tone indicative of the broadly changing mood of the text. Expressive changes in the organ accompaniment may add to the effectiveness of the chanting, but these should not be obtrusive. The accompaniment should be only an expressive background.

Except in large ecclesiastical establishments it is not expected that the choir will be able to chant the entire Psalter. Chanting is really a very difficult art, especially if such an extensive body as the entire Psalter is undertaken. For successful chanting, over-many psalms or psalm verses should not be used. Those that are used should come to be intimately familiar and devotionally expressive alike to chanters and to congregation. It is the task of religious education to bring this about on the part of the congregation. A corpus of worship, properly constituted, would include, together with other devotional material, those parts of the Psalter which are most significant religiously and are peculiarly fitted for use in the modern church service.

To be inspiring, chanting must be alive and meaningful. It must not be allowed to lapse into a mechanical routine. That notes are simple and words familiar does not insure chanting against becoming dull and lifeless. It must be kept animated by constant study and by an ever-renewed sensitiveness to the text. The chanted parts of a service should regularly be cared for and revivified at rehearsal.

CHOIR MUSIC, especially anthem music, is perhaps more likely than other forms of church music to become merely "music in church." This is not due to any inherent inability of its becoming genuine church music of the highest order, but to inadequate treatment of it. The practice of church music is often such as to cause the choir to be regarded objectively as a body of singers and choir music as a thing of merely musical pleasure. These tendencies may be counteracted to a very large degree by placing the choir in the church so that their office as agent in worship will be rightly assumed by the congregation, and by placing choir music in the church service so that it will be religiously significant.

The placement of the choir in the church is an influence of greater importance than it is generally credited with being in the attainment of genuine church music, especially that of the ecclesiastical order. There are three different general locations for the choir: first, in front facing the congregation—either up behind the minister or down at the side; second, in the rear gallery; and third, in the chancel, usually with the choir divided, the two sides facing each other. The first of these is the least desirable. It tends to accentuate the choir as a musical body to be listened to, inducing a relationship of performer and audience rather than that of fellow worshipers.

Another means of creating a right attitude towards the choir and choir music, both on the part of the choir itself and of the congregation, is by vesting the members of the choir and by providing regulations for their proper demeanor, both as individuals and as a body. Vestments serve at once to depersonalize the members of the choir and to impress upon choir and congregation alike the true character and function of church music. The conduct of the service and the manner of all those concerned with it are influences of a ceremonial order which are of great importance in promoting worship.

More important than either of these influences, however, is the placement of the anthem and other choir music in the service. As choir music is of an emotionally reflective character, it should be intimately related in mood and generally in thought also to those parts of the service with which it is associated. It needs a devotional setting, for the mood of devotion must have a considerable degree of continuity. Being emotionally reflective, the anthem naturally depends more upon what precedes it in the service than upon what follows it. Choir music may, however, be of such a character as to prepare impressively for that which succeeds it, as for instance, an anthem before a prayer. Another fact which should not be overlooked is that pertinency in the setting of anthems and other choir music in the service induces a right spirit for their performance.

CHOIR MUSIC is not infrequently taken to be a matter of sufferance by the congregation. Sometimes there is a distinct aversion to it. Unfortunately, it is regarded as being hostile to congregational music and not, as it should be, supplementary to it. This attitude may, in part at least, be occasioned by there frequently being too much choir music in a service; sometimes services seem to be over-loaded and even cluttered up with such music. And then again, antipathy to choir music may be occasioned by its lack of relevancy in the service, causing it thereby to be merely music in church. Dislike of choir music may also be occasioned by inadequate performance which precludes its being of devotional value in the service.

Excessive and persistent loudness is a common fault. Many choirs seem ever to be storming a citadel. They do not realize that it is fulness of choral tone rather than mere loudness which induces the sense of grandeur and sublimity. Excessive loudness is not always occasioned by expressional aspirations. Too often singers simply let themselves go; often it seems as if each part, or it may be each voice, is fighting for a hearing. Sometimes, however, but not always, they are incited to this by the director or by a flood of organ tone. It is a great mistake to regard vociferation as the ideal in vocal music, surely not in choir music.

Another common fault is that marks of expression are either little noted or are merely mechanically observed. Marks of expression, which are general indications by way of suggestion or explicit directions as to the character to be sought for the music, are parts of a musical composition as much as notes. They are to be interpreted expressionally, and not in such a way as to make those in the pews conscious that this or that direction in a printed page is being carried out—a *crescendo* or *rallentando* here or a contrast in volume of tone there. Then again, the vocal tone of choirs is often not as good as it ought to be. It should be as beautiful as possible, for tonal beauty is distinctly appropriate to religious worship.

Churches, furthermore, are frequently not as effective as they should be in their treatment of music. Some seem ever to be shifting from one type of choir music to another, or from choir music to congregational singing—and back, as if choir music and congregational music were alternatives and not supplementary forms. Then too, where a given type of choir is maintained there are in many instances needlessly frequent changes in personnel. It is not sufficiently realized that, other things being equal, permanency of personnel is desirable. To develop a unified and dependable ensemble and to build up a resourceful repertory take time. Frequent changes are detrimental to the morale of a choir and are discouraging to the director, who comes to feel that he is building upon sand and that his best efforts are constantly frustrated. These and other defects could easily be overcome by intelligent treatment of choir music.

CHOIR MUSIC has a high and worthy place in the realm of church music. It should be a means of giving spiritual beauty and increased spiritual vitality to worship, and not be merely a superficial accessory in the service, for it is within the power of music loftily to intensify religious consciousness and thought and to give utterance on a plane which words cannot reach.

MUSIC IN WORSHIP

True church music gives a sense of freedom and exaltation to the worshiper. It is a means of uplifting worship. In choir music, and in fact in all church music, it is not first and foremost the intrinsic quality of the music, though this is important, but the depth of devotion which it evokes and to which it gives expression that justifies its use in divine worship.

CHAPTER XII

ORGAN MUSIC

BOTH VOCAL and instrumental music find place in our church services. They are, however, most extensively used in combination rather than separately. But even so, unaccompanied vocal music and purely instrumental music are important forms of sacred music.

In mediaeval times unaccompanied vocal music was used almost exclusively. At that time, when as yet instrumental music had not attained considerable development or gained a substantial footing, the art of writing for unaccompanied voices reached its highest development. It is interesting to note in this connection that the Russian church has never used any but vocal music in its services; in fact, there are no organs in its churches. With the development of the modern art of musical composition and the perfecting of the modern organ, purely instrumental music has attained capabilities for aiding worship in ways far transcending those when the art of music was not in a fully developed stage and musical instruments were crude.

In the absence of words and the direction of thought which they are capable of giving, instrumental music in the church service has to depend upon the associational factor, concurrent and recall, and upon the ceremonial factor for attaining that conceptual element which is essential in church music. The problems and possibilities of instrumental church music are consequently quite different from those of vocal music. It is by perceiving and, in practice, securing conditions and circumstances in which it may attain religious significance, and by discerning the character of music and cultivating the spirit of performance which has special propriety and potency in religious worship, that we may secure effective instrumental church music. The devotional circumstances and manner of the use of instrumental music have very much to do with its becoming genuine church music.

In the modern church service there are usually two or three organ numbers: a prelude, a postlude, and possibly an offertory. The most important of these is the prelude, which is designed to gather up the spirit of the occasion in preparation for the service. Arresting attention and creating a mood, it opens the service. In current practice there are four rather distinct types of preludes. The simplest, found in some Episcopal churches, is very brief, without marked features, intended merely to obviate abruptness in beginning the service. Such a prelude, even though it is of but one or two minutes' duration, may do much to attune the congregation to worship. A second type, the one which is most common, is a prelude lasting from three to five minutes. A prelude of this type, in that it seeks to bring to stronger and deeper consciousness the attitude and spirit of worship, may be said to be a really constituent and important part of the service. Then there is the prelude, somewhat longer than the preceding, composed of a number of pieces, in which the purely musical element is pronounced. Preludes of this type, constituting a considerable musical period in which fairly quiet music is for the most part employed, are likely to be dull or sentimental or otherwise inapt. A wise selection and succession of compositions will, however, prevent this. As the fourth type, there is the pre-service recital. In this a very wide range of organ music may be used, exclusive of that which is secularly brilliant and gay or otherwise obviously inappropriate.

When more than a single composition is used, successive numbers should be appropriately contrasted and related as to mood and character. Key relationship should also be given consideration. Continuity and effectiveness in church music is gained by successive numbers being so related as to key that they succeed each other responsively—as for instance, a composition in G major being followed by one in C major or minor, in E flat major or E minor, rather than by one in a foreign key such as D flat and A flat major or F minor. Thereby the feeling that one is hearing a series of "set pieces," concertwise, is reduced and possibly wholly avoided.

Of the four types of preludes, the first two are wholly intended to enhance the service, while the latter two, especially the last, have in large measure the purpose of attracting attendance by musical offerings. The second type of prelude, that running from three to five minutes, is the one generally to be preferred. It is sizable enough to be significant, yet not so long as to call for a series of pieces which, if consisting of quiet compositions, might tend to sameness or sentimentality or, if composed of varied contrasted items, gives an air of concert performance. Furthermore, it covers a period not so extensive as to constitute this preliminary music a thing in itself, and by virtue of concentrating attention and creating a mood of worship, it preserves the character of a genuine pre-lude to the service.

Organ music at the beginning of the service should focus and concentrate attention and create a right atmosphere for worship. It should be contemplative in character, not diverting; solemn, but not sombre or dull. Generally it should be subdued, though it may sometimes in its course rise to considerable volume. The impressive power of the organ is felt most distinctly in the prelude. Its composure, its sustained grandeur, its incomparable calm, its majesty tend to develop a mood of worship and devotion and to lead from the feverish, trivial and routine to the eternal, noble, and inspiring. How mystically solemn is the soft deep tone of the pedal! How arresting the instealing harmonies! How conducive to worship the contemplative movement of melodic inner parts! And as the prelude proceeds, what a sense of dignity, elevation and nobility! And finally, as the tone dies away, a moment of stillness, unspeakably impressive, profoundly moving, uplifting!

Although the prelude should generally be more or less subdued in character, giving a sense of composure and confidence, it should never sound timid or tame. It should always begin rather quietly. Even on festival days, like Christmas or Easter, when it may be elaborate and jubilant, the prelude should not be begun with a loud chord, abruptly, but should be led into by a *crescendo,* or by a brief bit of preliminary music. Impressiveness and exalted solemnity or tenderness and the sense of peace should characterize the organ music at the beginning of the service—the prelude is properly something more than a pleasant piece of music played before the service. In general, the contrapuntal style and texture is better than the melodically homophonic. Thematic organ music is more desirable for use in the church service than that which is lyrical in character. But the adoption of a style is not the whole matter; mere contrapuntal music is not sacred. The ideal service prelude is self-effacing art. The spirit which it imparts is definitely greater than itself.

An ideal form of service prelude, at least for German or Lutheran congregations, is found in the German chorale prelude, which has as its basis a church theme enfolded in free meditative preluding. Here is pertinent and effective suggestion, the chorale theme with its familiar words affording the conceptual element. The out about the use of German chorale preludes, except in German or Lutheran churches, is that the choral themes, which give suggestion, are in large measure unfamiliar, and hence preludes founded upon them are devoid of that significance which is given by association and suggestion. Without this key the preludes are not very effective, save as the free parts are contemplatively conceived and developed; without the key of the chorale itself many chorale preludes are dull and uninteresting. In England and America there has been in recent years a considerable output of preludes based on hymn tunes. Unfortunately many of the tunes used by English composers are unfamiliar to American congregations.

There is, of course, a large body of excellent organ music which is of such a character as to create, with the aid of religiously ceremonial and associational influences, an atmosphere conducive to worship. Each piece should be accepted on its distinctive merits for church use.

Although the character of the music and the manner of performance are very important, the effectiveness of the prelude in the church service does not depend wholly upon musical considerations. There are factors in church music other than the purely musical—the conceptual, the ceremonial, and the associational. Failure of the prelude to realize its possibilities is often due in large measure to the absence of regard of these —for instance, regard for the church as a consecrated place, or, if you prefer, a place of consecration. Where the church is not felt to be distinctly a consecrated place, the members of the congregation maintain more than they otherwise would a secular attitude of mind and a secular manner of conduct until the very beginning of the liturgical service. This tends, unwittingly, to prevent the prelude from becoming a genuine part of the service. For those to whom the church is a consecrated place, the service in large measure begins when they enter the building, take their seats and bow their heads in prayer. The attitude of mind and spirit which this conception and this practice engender creates a condition in which the prelude may attain religious significance. In gathering up and bringing to clearer consciousness the spirit of the place in preparation for the service, the prelude becomes an integral part of the service.

The conduct of those within the church is also an important influence affecting the attainment of religious value in the prelude. It is generally at the time of the prelude or in connection with it that those other than the organist who have to do with the conduct of the service take their positions. The manner of entrance of the officiating clergyman and church musicians, whether in procession or not, and their conduct thereafter are very likely to add to or subtract from the service. Being in the foreground, their movements are noticeable. If the choir members stroll in or listlessly move about, or if when seated they turn their bodies or heads more or less conspicuously, to say nothing of conversing, finding books and places in them, things are far from being what they ought to be. In many churches there is too little consideration of matters of this sort. On the other hand, too great precision and formality are undesirable. Sometimes there is veritable clockwork at the beginning of the service, as when the congregation hears three strokes of the bell as a signal, or it may be a buzzer, and then, instanter—the organ. The prelude then appears to be nothing more than mechanically starting the cogs. Ceremonial matters at the beginning of the service should be such that the prelude may become a veritable and natural part of it. During the fifteen minutes before the liturgical beginning of the service, there should be silence in the church and no unnecessary movement. All arrangements for the occasion should have been completed previously.

Attempt is sometimes made to make the prelude an integral part of the service by inserting it within the service area. Instead of having it precede the stipulated time for the beginning of the service proper, it is begun at that time and is constituted the first number in the service, the minister and congregation being in waiting. Trying thus mechanically and forcibly to make the music an integral part of the service is ineffective. The time of the prelude is likely to become an inactive period, one in which the inert congregation feels that attempt is being made to enforce an organ number as a part of the service. It is far better to obviate untoward conditions for the realization of the function of the prelude by the creation of a high sense of reverence for the church as the House of God and place of prayer and by preserving in the service a demeanor in accord with this.

A right attitude as to the church and its services on the part of the congregation, clergy and church musicians is of great importance in affecting not only the prelude but also the entire first part of the service. The presence at the beginning of the service of a secular spirit, foreign to it and not definitely in consonance with it, is an initial mistake. It induces a condition in which what are termed "opening exercises" seem calculated and called upon, often unsuccessfully, to counteract. It weakens the service, causing waste of time and effort. Sometimes, indeed, the secular spirit is not fully counteracted and the spirit of worship is but little realized in the service. Now that churches are more and more providing themselves with parish houses, where secularly-social activities have place, the church building itself should be exclusively and intensively devoted to the attainment of worship. To do this—and it can readily be done—would in many instances constitute a great reform, enhancing the religious power of the church through the stronger devotional character of its services.

A prelude, which in itself may be excellent, is furthermore often greatly diminished in value by being unhappily related to the liturgical beginning of the service. There should be a definite understanding between minister and organist as to the exact time the liturgical service is to begin, and the organist should time and select his music so that it fits the period and be careful to begin the playing so that the prelude will be terminated at the right moment. It is unfortunate for the organist to cut a composition in the middle, or for the service to have to wait for the prelude to be brought to a close; and on the other hand, it is unfortunate for the organist to have to hang back, filling in as best he may with a time-killing improvisation. Such a gap and filling in of a period of uncertain length with inconsequential, rambling harmonies and listless modulations gives a sense of halting and delay which puts a damper on the service at its beginning.

In services of the evangelical sort—in church music of the evangelical type—the prelude will naturally have greater warmth and buoyancy and a stronger physically emotional character than in services of the distinctly ecclesiastical sort; but, on the other hand, there will be less sense of awe, less quiet, reverent contemplation. The character of the music and the spirit of its performance will not be so far removed from the secular as in the case of the ecclesiastical type of service and church music; yet, by its arousing a larger degree of distinctly social consciousness and creating a strong emotional state in the individual, it may induce a condition favorable for consideration of things of a religious nature and for response to religious appeal.

THE POSTLUDE is intrinsically less influential in the service than the prelude. At the time of the postlude the attitude of the congregation is quite different from that during the prelude. The congregation is breaking up, the service is receding, attention is being dispersed. Some are departing, bent on getting home; many remain to greet and chat with friends; others still, shy of church courtesies or feeling awkward to remain when others generally are leaving, go out with the flux; a few, possibly, may wait and really listen to the postlude. That portion of the congregation which is retiring is doing so without expectation of hearing the postlude to the end, while those who remain are for the most part wholly engaged in conversation. In these circumstances the postlude is only casually listened to and is of comparatively little account.

But though the postlude may add comparatively little to the service, it may subtract much. Coming in with a deafening crash after a solemn moment, or by immediately transforming the church musically into a concert hall, or by asserting a mood quite foreign to that which pervaded the close of the service, it may largely dispel the good impression of the service. This maladjustment of the postlude has long been recognized. Addison, or one of his associates, in the *Spectator* of March 28, 1712, writes of "good thoughts and dispositions" having "all been in a moment dissipated by a merry jig from the organ loft." Let us hope that things are not quite so bad with us! They need not be.

The postlude comes too late in the service to initiate a new section. Nevertheless, by extending the mood of the service and giving it an increased sense of permanence, as well as by avoiding an abrupt ending, it may furnish a worthy and appropriate termination to the service. For the postlude to be of greatest religious value, the liturgical service must have been brought to a close in a ceremonial and dignified manner; after the blessing or benediction, there should inevitably be a moment of quiet, reverent silence.

Postludes, or after-service music, to use a more inclusive term, may be of four kinds. The most common is that which follows directly upon the close of the liturgical service. Though it need not be so, postludes of this sort are frequently shocking, unceremoniously bursting in the moment the benediction has been pronounced, their purpose being thought of as that of "playing the people out." Instead of abruptly breaking in, the organist should allow a moment or so of reverent silence, followed by a brief musical preparation for the postlude—a transitional period beginning softly and gradually but rapidly working into the final music of the service, which, while it may be bright and joyous, should above all things have a majesty befitting the place and act of worship.

In order that this type of postlude may be well-articulated and appropriate to the particular service, it is necessary that the organist know beforehand what is to be the general character of the end of the service. In many cases it is the character of the final hymn which has special significance. In planning the postlude the organist ought to know what this hymn after the sermon is to be, for being the last considerable musical item in the liturgical service, it is so near the postlude that its impression tends to carry over into this. Its key and rhythm, its general mood and character should be taken into consideration by the organist in selecting the postlude. The last hymn and the postlude are points of musical contact to be carefully adjusted; if they are not, there is likely to be more or less of a clash.

Another kind of postlude is one which follows the liturgical service somewhat remotely, not with the immediacy of the first type. In this case the postlude is only slenderly connected with the service. Begun after a sufficient interim has been allowed for the service somewhat to recede and as the people are beginning to leave the church, a postlude, joyous but dignified and reverent, may give a trail of brightness and exaltation to the service—an afterglow—and impart to the church as a sanctuary a sense of permanent warmth and radiance.

A third type is that in which the postlude is made a definite and separate item in the program. In this case the congregation is requested to remain seated while an extended organ composition of marked distinction is performed. This treatment of the final music of the service is one of special and not regular occurrence.

Lastly, there is the possibility of a short organ recital following the service. After the morning service a recital would hardly be effective, but after the evening service a brief recital may be very fitting. In the evening hour, at close of day, there is a mystical atmosphere which invites to after-service music. Such a recital, which may be of occasional or of somewhat regular occurrence, will in general be characterized by serenity and peace, but it should not be devoid of the sense of majesty and strength. Sentimentality, on the one hand, and boisterousness on the other, are alike inapt. An interval of a few moments should be allowed after the termination of the service proper in order that those who do not care to stay may leave the church and that quiet be secured for the peaceful enjoyment of the music.

In recent times, following the revived appreciation of the chorale prelude as embodying a sound principle in the field of organ service-music, there has been an increase in the composition of hymn-tune postludes as well as preludes. A postlude founded upon one of the hymn tunes used in the service, especially that of the last hymn, may be made a most appropriate and effective ending for a service. It is not well, however, to use a hymn-tune postlude regularly, lest it comes to be conventionally expected and its influence be thereby lessened. There is, of course, a large body of other music—movements from organ sonatas, individual organ compositions, and transcriptions of certain oratorio choruses—upon which chief reliance should be placed. Much of this is superior to many hymn-tune postludes, not all of which are of a high level.

For attaining the full function of the postlude, as well as that of the prelude, the character of the music and the spirit of performance are important, but they are not all that is requisite. In both instances there are things beyond the control of the organist which are needful. Clergy and congregation have a part in creating and maintaining conditions wherein both prelude and postlude may be of value in promoting worship.

THE PERIOD of the offertory varies widely in character, ranging from an almost entirely financial interval to a sacramental period. These features are sometimes mixed and strangely intermingled. At the time of the offertory there is generally some kind of music—an organ composition or improvisation, a solo, an anthem, or a congregational hymn. The music at this point tends more than elsewhere to be "music in church" rather than "church music." The necessary movements of the collectors, the passing of plates, the clinking of coins and the general stir do not make a favorable occasion for devotional church music. Almost inevitably the period has more or less the nature of an intermission. The character of the music currently heard in this section of the service is quite various. There may be sweet and delicate organ music, a florid anthem, or a vocal solo, frequently more or less sentimental or sensationally dramatic, the soloist in some instances standing out and having all the characteristics of a concert performer—except the bow; or on the other hand, there may be impressive organ music, an anthem of religious quality, or a congregational hymn. Curiously enough, there is in many non-liturgical churches, and sometimes in liturgical churches as well, a glorified presentation of the alms, so that this becomes the most distinctly ceremonial event in the entire service.

As the offertory, more than any other music in the service, is liable to have a secular spirit, care should be taken to minimize this and to avoid its becoming contagious, causing the other music of the service to become likewise merely "music in church."

A too sudden starting of the offertory music accentuates its filling-in character, detracting from whatever dignity and graciousness it is capable of acquiring. This applies to both vocal and instrumental music. Being somewhat incidental, offertory music should be introduced incidentally. Preferably the composition selected should be comparatively short for the period rather than long. It is better for the organist to improvise a minute or so while the ushers are finishing than to have them and the congregation kept in waiting while some piece is being brought to completion. This is especially so if the music is instrumental. Furthermore, the early termination of a set piece may give the sense of expectancy and an adjusting improvisation may give ease to the proceedings. In case the organist is so situated that he cannot see when the ushers are ready to advance, there should be an agreement that the rising of the minister to receive the offering be signal both for ushers and for organist.

In ADDITION to the prelude and postlude and possibly offertory, there may well be improvised organ music to weld together various items of the service so that there shall be no awkwardness or abruptness in their succession and also at the same time give the service increased unity.

The church service should be something more than an accumulation of parts. Musical sections, if isolated items, tend to be regarded objectively—and thereby become "music in church." Worship has continuity; it is a movement of the Soul. It must have an attitudinal background. Thoughts may flash before us, but reflective aspiration, communion and dedication require a certain duration and continuity of mood. Organ music may be of great value in gaining this continuity and in effecting transition of mood.

Improvised transitional passages may not only obviate gaps and incongruous successions in the proceedings, they may heighten the significance and character of the parts which they mediate. Take, for instance, a transition from the prelude to the Doxology: in churches where this liturgical beginning of the service obtains, a modulatory transition from the prelude may be such as not only to avoid distressing key relationships but also to give an impressive setting to the Doxology. So also, as has been suggested, a short, interlude-like passage may effectively introduce a postlude of fine character. If, at the reception of the offering, there is a choral item—the Doxology or the chant, "All things come of Thee"—a well-ordered extemporized passage after the offertory music may effectively lead to the Doxology or chant. Again, in case the versicles ending with "The Lord's Name be praised" are followed by a chant in another key, a modulatory extemporized passage may not only connect them, but also, in musically spacing them by a slight interval, may heighten the individuality of both versicle and canticle. In some churches there is improvised music while late-comers are receiving attention, also while the congregation are finding their places for the responsive reading. The first of these, if it must be, should be as brief as possible; the second is entirely unnecessary and superfluous.

But interludial passages ought not to be too numerous or too extended. Often they are both; the parts of the service are glued together, much as the notes in organ-playing were in times past when unvarying legato was the rule. Moments of silence between items in the service are natural and desirable; often they may be ceremonially expressive. Points of silence here and there may, as it were, punctuate the service. Sometimes it seems as if ministers and musicians feel that there must be perpetual sound. In order not to have a musical number end awkwardly, it may be well for the organist to taper it off, but tapering off every item is a tedious mannerism detracting from the life of the service. Now and then, indeed, a definite break, with a fresh start, may be desirable.

Extemporized music may furthermore be effective in connection with silent devotional periods. The mood of a period of expressive religious silence may be somewhat extended through the use of music: as the impressiveness of ceremonial silence is waning, incoming music may gather up its mood and strengthen its impressiveness, heightening and deepening the sense of adoration and reverence, intimacy and awe.

Organists should develop their improvisational abilities. This can be done by study and experimentation—but let the experimentation be done mostly by themselves and not wholly in public. It is in improvising short modulatory passages and interludes, and not extended preludes or postludes, that the ordinary organist should be proficient. It is, so to speak, ability in conversation rather than power in oratorical address that he should seek. His extemporized transitions and modulations during the service should be clear and coherent; if he is not able to make them anything more than clumsy, rambling, inane meanderings, they should not be attempted. There is obvious need of more attention to this matter. To improvise effectively in the service, the organist should have a good working knowledge of harmony, counterpoint, and musical form; this should be of the keyboard rather than the paper sort, for it is to be used in action and not in elaborated composition. Organists will find that improvisation in two and three parts, and also the use of an occasional unison or octave, gives a desirable relief from persistent four-part harmony. They will also find that the upper part of the manual range, from middle C up two octaves, is in many organs an especially effective area for extemporizing in devotional periods. The various transition sections of the service should be of musical material which in rhythm, melody, and type of harmony is related to the more formally composed music with which they are associated.

THE GREAT improvement in the construction of the organ in recent years has made it a much more plastic instrument than it was formerly. The modern electric action with its numerous couplers and combination pistons and other facilities has rendered the organ flexible to a degree formerly undreamed of.

This makes possible the avoidance of the tiresomeness of long protracted passages for full organ, as well as the attainment of a much more varied and nicely graded registration in the quieter passages. Without creating a feeling of slump, the body of tone in comparatively loud compositions may now be naturally and unobtrusively reduced from the maximum, relieving the disagreeable insistence of the full organ. A long continued absolute *fortissimo* is as inartistic as it is irritating. When the peak has been made, there should be a recession of tone. The peak may be pointed or it may be broad; in choir music and in the organ music of the church it will probably be the latter which is particularly pertinent. Climaxes and points of relief are as desirable in loud passages as are expressive nuances in the softer sections. It is strange how often musicians who are sensitive to the beauties of delicate tone color fail to realize how distressing to the listener is a persistent and unvaryingly loud stretch of sound. Organists should constantly remind themselves that "people have ears," and govern themselves accordingly. With all the facilities which the modern organist has at hand, there is no excuse for his imposing even on a retreating congregation postludes which are annoying by their persistent loudness and blatancy.

Of all musical instruments the organ is the least standardized. Church organs vary greatly in size and also in the details of their specifications. This fact naturally affects both organ composition and the performance of organ music. The organ composer is less able than the orchestral or piano composer to score his music with precision, for the stops on different organs are not of uniform number or character, stops of the same name varying considerably in power and even in quality. This limits the definiteness of expressive direction on the part of the composer and increases the requisitions of the organist as an interpreter. Dynamic and tonal directions given by the composer can only be more or less general; they are almost always to be taken as suggestions to be worked out in detail by the organist according to the expressive capabilities of his particular instrument. The judgment and ingenuity of the organist has constantly to be exercised in this matter of registration.

On account of the mechanical constitution of the instrument, organ music is of a less minutely sensitive and changeful character than orchestral or piano music. It is broader and less impassioned. It has a sustained majesty, serenity, and elevation which is all its own. That grandeur and mystical quiet which it is capable of attaining, that elevated composure and impressiveness which may characterize it, together with its stimulating sweep are unique qualities which make it especially suited for use in religious worship. These capabilities of expression should be attentively made use of by the organist in the service.

THE ORGAN MUSIC heard in our churches has wide diversity of character and mood, ranging from the forbiddingly severe to the luscious. Some, though not all, professional organists are inclined to use music which is learned and technically exacting, others that which is severe along the lines of the ecclesiastically traditional. Many use music which is suave and bland, sensuous and ear-tickling, still others music which is simply dull and stupid. In selecting organ music the organist should take into consideration cultural and traditional church-music backgrounds. These vary in different churches. They are the product of the past; the organist, however, is an active agent in the present. His music should always have dignity and impressiveness.

Whatever is played in the service should be within the technical proficiency of the organist and capable of adequate realization with the instrument at his command. He should not struggle through in public what he cannot properly perform; in loud passages there should be steadiness and firmness and in soft passages repose and composure. Nor should he select music which is not suited to his instrument. Much of the best organ music requires a really large and resourceful instrument for its effective performance. With the great diversity there is in organs there will be no strict uniformity as to the feasibility of this or that organ composition. Each piece must be chosen upon its own merits and with reference to the condition of its intended use.

The all too common lack of regard for the prelude and the other organ music in the service may not be due primarily to the congregation, the service, or the minister, but to the organist himself. Many organists make hasty and careless selection of their organ music and give it an indifferent performance. No wonder they complain of lack of appreciation! For the congregation to regard the prelude and the other organ music in the service attentively and seriously, it should be made worthy of such regard by its character and performance.

The style and idiom of sacred music should conform to the inner thought and emotion in religion. Organ music, as compared with choir or congregational music, is closely allied to architecture. The organ is a part of the church building and organ music in the service a permeating influence rather than an active agent in the proceedings. There should always be about the organ music of the church a certain elevation and a spaciousness which is characteristic of the church and its services. The prelude, for instance, should never be a restless, agitated affair, the tempo constantly changing, the volume of tone inconsequentially fluctuating; nor in quiet music should soft solo stops be used in a changeful, finicky way in display of their varied color—*vox humana, celeste, four-foot flute, clarinet.* There should be breadth and nobility of style and artistic self-restraint. The impression of its being a performance should be reduced to a minimum.

Improvement in the musical appreciation and responsiveness of the congregation is to be effected by the discreet introduction of a better type of church music. One excellent way of doing this is by using a superior and distinctive type of organ music —say, music of simple and significant character in modal or Gregorian style—in places in the service where the devotional mood is strong, at impressive points where there is an organ interlude or response and in the communion service. Then such music will distinctly be felt to be right and desirable. This gets at the problem of church music through worship, which is the best procedure. Later such organ music, still of simple composure and not overlong, may gradually be introduced at the time of the prelude and postlude. This use of organ music will in turn prepare for a better type of choir music.

A DISTINCT advance has been made in recent years in the ideals and standards of organ-playing as well as in the construction of the instrument. There is now more beauty and expressiveness than there was commonly in the past. There is rhythm, accent and phrasing secured through a very subtle shortening and lengthening of time values and gradations of *staccato, legato,* and *tenuto.* The style of playing in the church service is necessarily somewhat different from that in a recital. In service-playing the phrasing, while being clear, will be less sharp and pointed than in recital-playing, and the registration, while being colorful, will be less highly contrasted in its make-up. Instead of brilliancy or piquancy, breadth and dignity will be sought. This difference between recital and service organ music should lie both in the style of performance and in type of music. Some music will be appropriate and effective for use in both a recital and the service. The style of performance in the two instances will, however, probably be somewhat different.

With the increase of the use of the organ in concert recitals and elsewhere, differentiation between organ music suited to sacred use and that which is of secular character becomes more and more necessary. The organ is no longer solely a church instrument. It may go the way of the harp as "a characteristic religious musical instrument"—at least to a degree. Much current organ music is merely pleasing and diverting, and properly so; not a little is dryly scientific and dull, some is capricious. And there is other organ music which is aesthetically excellent, often affording opportunity for the technical and artistic display of the performer. But in selecting organ music for the service and in performing it, the organist should hold the attainment of the spirit of worship as his controlling and guiding consideration.

It will readily be granted that not all music which is excellent as music is suitable for church use. To be appropriate it should be such as will move one religiously. That which has secular association is not proper for church use unless such secular association is with instrumental compositions which are inherently of a religious character rather than of secular interest and delight. It is to be hoped that the several types of organ music may be more and more differentiated and that the special field of ecclesiastical organ music will receive its full quota of attention from composers, who may add to its store and thereby make essential contribution to the attainment of genuine church music.

CHAPTER XIII

THE DIRECTOR

THE EFFICIENCY and effectiveness of church music depends more upon the director than upon any other person. Others may make practical contribution both vital and prominent—some members of the choir may indeed be veritable towers of strength, and the director gratefully appreciates them—but it is the director himself who by virtue of the duties delegated to him largely determines the aim of church music in the church he serves and it is he who in large measure must attain it. Upon him rests the responsibility of choosing the material to be used, both as to its appropriateness and its practicability; he effects the preparation of the music for the services and determines its interpretation; and in the service his is the guiding hand and animating spirit. Every director has restrictions in the means available for his purpose. It is, however, incumbent upon him to make the most of what he has to do with and to discern and develop the potentialities of his charge. His vision and perception, his ideals and competency become in time those of his choir. The limitations of the choir are to a large extent those of the director. A choir cannot well be better than its director.

The office of director is usually combined with that of organist. In some churches, however, one of the singers acts in the capacity of director, while in others a special conductor is appointed as leader of the choir. The relative desirability of these three possibilities is an important matter for consideration.

Generally it will be found that the combining of the offices of organist and director is by far the most workable plan. Organists as a class are more broadly educated musically than most other musicians, usually being more acquainted with musical theory and having a larger working knowledge of harmony and counterpoint. Of musicians at the present time, they alone have occasion in their work to make practical use of this knowledge and exercise their skill in improvising. From the nature and extent of his work, the organist is likely to have a more comprehensive perception of the various factors entering into church music, and during the service he is in more sensitive touch with the choir and congregation than any other person. As most choir music is organ-accompanied, he is constantly called upon to exercise artistic judgment in accompanying the choir. More than any other person, he may effectively relate instrumental and choral parts. An organist-director may do this best, not only because he is a free agent but also because, as no two organs are alike, he comes to know better than anyone else the possibilities of his particular instrument.

Since nowadays the console may be placed anywhere in the church, the organist no longer has to sit up against the organ, his back to the singers, but may have his console so located as to afford him an excellent opportunity to hear his instrument in organ music and in association with the choir, and also to admit his giving the singers, quite unobtrusively, whatever signals or conducting guidance he may wish. Direction during the service should be slight. Provided the necessary preliminary work has been done in the choir room, and later perhaps in the church with the organ, even large choirs need very little direction in the service. The choir as a vocal body should be self-subsistent and not be in need of obvious leadership or coercion from the organ bench.

In passing, it should be noted that freedom in locating the console has in many instances been unwisely used. In some churches the organist is placed at the front in the body of the church facing the choir so that, presumably, he may better direct them. This arrangement, instead of being a benefit, is a handicap. All the movements he makes in manipulating his instrument and adjusting his music, and whatever motions he may have occasion to make in directing the choir are in clear view of everybody, so that his freedom of action is restricted. Organists, organ builders, architects, and church committees should realize the desirability of placing the console in an inconspicuous situation and in a position where the organist may have the opportunity of accurately estimating the effect of both choir and organ music and have freedom in controlling his forces.

There are various other considerations in favor of the organist being director. For one thing, the office of organist-director is attractive to a proficient organist. Again, an organist who is really competent hardly cares to place himself under the direction of another unless that person has a much wider musical knowledge and experience than he. Furthermore, when the duties of organist and director are united in one person there is this great advantage, there can then be no possibility of any misunderstanding or friction between organist and director!

Sometimes a singer is made the director. Such a one will tend to regard the choir more distinctly as a vocal body and make the voices relatively more prominent in the ensemble. Greater relative prominence of the vocal element may not, however, guarantee greater expressiveness through it. In its raw estate, vocal music is no more valuable than instrumental. Choral expressiveness has possibilities of which many singers, as well as many organists, are not aware. It is sometimes said of organists that they are by training and interest unduly instrumental and that their conceptions and ideals in church music are not sufficiently vocal. Undoubtedly there is a tendency for the organist to think in terms of the organ rather than in terms of the voice. But what we may sometimes feel to be an overloud accompaniment may have been used, discreetly or indiscreetly, to cover up the inadequacies of the choir. On the other hand, singers as well as organists are likely to overdo. In his anxiety to gain desired results, a singer in charge of a choir may often overstress his individual participation; in endeavoring to hold things together or to attain a certain vigor or detail in expression, he may sing so that his voice is insistently and disagreeably prominent. It may be expected of a singer-director that he will give general voice-training to those in his charge, but such a possibility is not always to be counted on: an organist as well as a singer may become proficient to do this.

The third type of choir director is the conductor-director. Usually such conducting as is necessary in the service may readily be done unobtrusively by the organist from the organ bench; he may be placed so as to command the view of his choir either directly or through the use of a mirror so that to the congregation there will seem to be no directing whatsoever. Preparation of choir music should have been completed in the rehearsal room, and directing during the service should be reduced to an absolute minimum, both in fact and in appearance. It is undesirable for the congregation to be conscious of any directing, either by the organist from the bench or by an independent director. The movements in directing are more of musical than of devotional significance. Visible direction of a choir tends inevitably to draw attention to the music as such, to produce "music in church" rather than genuine church music.

THE SCOPE and character of the director's duties vary in different churches and with different types of choir. They are of two general kinds, musical and managerial. Musical duties are common to all, while managerial duties vary widely, in some cases being comparatively slight and in others quite extensive, requiring the expenditure of much time and effort. Choir schemes range from a soloist or quartet to an elaborate lay-out in which the director recruits and maintains a large adult chorus, a children's choir, and possibly an intermediate choir, and it may be he has also supervision of the music for all services of whatever sort. In the latter case, a director, who may or may not be an organist, is appointed to develop various choral groups, and for such services receives a large part of the appropriation for music. In small churches and in those having

173

comparatively small choirs, the importance of the work of the director—in these cases mostly musical in character—is apt to be little recognized. Someone has to serve in this capacity, and it generally comes about that the musical direction and care of the choir devolve upon one of its older or more experienced members, who is slightly, if at all, remunerated for this service.

In the making of appointments to the various choir positions there are differences in practice. In the Episcopal church, for instance, the appointment of the director is generally lodged with the rector, possibly in conjunction with a music committee, while in other churches it is commonly in the hands of the music committee. Responsibility for the management of the music in its details is in most churches delegated by the committee to the director whom they have appointed. Choir appointments of any considerable importance should in small churches preferably be made by the committee, who, however, should act with the advice of the director; but in larger churches having a chorus choir, they may often best be handled by the director, for in such churches the director will presumably be much more competent in passing judgment than in a smaller parish and the appointments will be more numerous, those to minor positions probably being fairly frequent. Whatever the arrangement, the director should be paid a definite salary for his services, and not be given a lump sum, from which he may extract the utmost, as has sometimes been done. Payments, except those of a petty sort, should, so far as possible, be made directly by the treasurer to those having salaried appointments.

THE REHEARSAL is one of the prime means of attaining effective church music. It may seem strange to have to say this, but to many rehearsing seems to be regarded as something either superfluous, or not particularly necessary. Some think that people are naturally musical—and that is all there is to it; they look on things musical as not needing cultivation. Not infrequently there is lack of perception on the part of the director, as well as of others, as to what is real excellence in church music.

There are in general three characteristic ways of conducting rehearsals commonly to be found in church choirs.

First, there are directors who leave everything to the eleventh hour, and then scramble. Lazy and indifferent, they trust to the spur of the moment—an uncertain and unsubstantial reliance. Their way is to "try an anthem over" once or twice, or to "run something through" just before the service. To their minds it is sufficient for the choir and organist barely to know the notes, generally of something simple and commonplace. They think that when notes are learned all is done. In many instances such choirs do not even know the notes with certainty. They give the impression of "feeling their way"—as indeed they are, though they may not suspect that others are conscious of that fact. Neither do they realize how relieved others are when the number is over! Such choirs do not sing with spirit and expression. How can they? They add little, if anything, to the service; often they are a detraction.

Second, there are directors who concentrate effort exclusively on the music for the Sunday immediately coming. Living from hand to mouth, such directors offer fare of a generally inferior quality. The immediately obtainable is of necessity sought, and this is likely to be done irrespective of real worth.

Third, there are directors who have their work planned ahead and laid out so that there is no sense of rush. The music is selected with deliberation and care and is given adequate preparation. Through rehearsal in successive weeks worthy compositions are thoroughly mastered and made so intimately familiar that their performance becomes inspiring. Such music may be repeated with deepening regard on the part of the choir and with increased profit to the congregation. Through such a procedure a valuable and permanent repertory is built up, and choir music is put on a substantial and effective basis.

REHEARSALS should be held each week and at a regular time so that the members of the choir may plan to reserve this period for the purpose. Changes ought never to be made except for urgent reasons, for it is generally difficult to shift a rehearsal without seriously impairing it. In this matter the church should co-operate by not allowing conflicting activities to be scheduled for the regular choir rehearsal period.

Rehearsals should begin on time. That this may be accomplished, the director must set the example for punctuality by always himself being ahead of time and having everything in readiness. All music to be used should have been selected and copies be at hand; it should never appear to the choir members that they have arrived too early. Nothing is so tempting to tardiness, and justifying it, as to find the director not ready and to realize that had one been on time, the interval would have been wasted. On the other hand, nothing induces promptness so much as for a late member to find that the rehearsal is already in progress and that others are conscious of the work being held up or interrupted by his or her lateness. Sometimes, of course, it is useless to begin a rehearsal at the stated time, for there may not be even a sufficient number to work with. But if possible, a start of some kind should be made—a part-rehearsal may sometimes be undertaken. Rehearsals should also end on time. The director may sometimes be able to complain of tardiness by lamenting at the close of the rehearsal its not ending on time because it did not begin on time. He should, however, always realize that his ability in conducting the rehearsal has much to do with the possibility of its ending on time.

Irregularity in attendance, as was said in an earlier chapter, is one of the greatest sources of weakness in the chorus choir, and the despair of the choirmaster. Some members come to the rehearsal but not to the service, while others, as is more frequently the case, are not present at rehearsal but appear at the service. The smaller the choir the more disastrous is this irregularity of attendance. Many large choirs have a rule that those who have not attended the rehearsal may not sing at the service, an excellent rule, if it is possible to adhere to it and yet have a sufficient number of singers for the service. In many instances it might be impossible of enforcement without seriously impairing the service. Where the rule can be enforced there may be fewer singers at the service, but there will be a compensating gain in sureness and stability. With a fluctuating attendance it may be impossible to carry on effectively. In every choir there ought to be an agreement on the part of members to attend a minimum of seventy-five per cent of rehearsals and services. A record of attendance should be kept and report be made periodically at rehearsal. Delinquents will then find that they are holding down the attendance average and realize that those who are constant strongly disparage this. As a consequence, they are likely either to amend their ways or withdraw from the choir.

The quarters in which rehearsals are held should be bright and cheery, well-lighted and well-aired. All music to be used ought to be definitely selected before the rehearsal time. No portion of the period should be wasted in picking out something to sing, or in trying over this and that bit of music. Waste of time and dispersion of attention caused by defective methods of distributing and collecting music during rehearsal should be obviated. Especially in large choirs the use of an envelope for each member containing all the music to be practiced will expedite matters. If the various numbers are arranged in the envelope in the order in which they are to be taken up, all possible confusion and delay will be avoided. Every church which has a considerable choir should have a music cabinet and card catalogue, and each piece of music should have its catalogue number marked on it. Copies desired for use can then be immediately procured from the cabinet and at the close of the rehearsal quickly assorted and returned to their respective envelopes. This system is economical of time and saves the music from needless wear and tear.

Besides selecting all the music beforehand, the director ought to make himself intimately familiar with it. He should know the notes of the voice-parts, so that mistakes may be quickly detected and corrected; he should also anticipate places which will probably be troublesome and devise means of mastering them. Furthermore, he should formulate in his mind the ideal expression and interpretation of the music to be rehearsed. By conscientiously doing these things he will increase his own competency as well as conduct his rehearsals more efficiently. The more competent the choirmaster becomes, the more interesting will the rehearsal be to the members of the choir, and the more effective the choir music in the service.

Usually there are various kinds of music to be rehearsed and various sorts of work to be accomplished. Anthems, responses, chants and hymn tunes are to be taken up. Variety of material and different kinds of work make it readily possible for a choir rehearsal to become a stimulating and diversified practice. Care must be taken, however, lest a diversified rehearsal become a diffused rehearsal. Rehearsals should never be allowed to appear desultory or lacking in definite accomplishment. In general, a certain broad order should be followed. Some things are naturally done best in one part of the period and others in another. A flexible routine suited to the work to be done is both helpful to the director and agreeable to the choir.

It is best to begin with something fairly familiar and rather extended, and to end with something distinctive and particularly interesting to the choir, thereby gaining an impetus at the beginning and a sense of achievement at its close. Details are most easily attended to when the rehearsal has gotten under way. In taking up a new composition or renewing an old one, it is generally wise, unless it is an exceedingly long one, to have it sung through in its entirety, the director meanwhile noting all places which are incorrect or unsteady or should for other reasons be given special attention. An anthem should never be run through again and again merely in hope it will go better and better. All practice should be intelligent and purposive, the director always making it perfectly clear to the choir just what is sought and how it may be secured. This is most readily attained through brief critical comments, not through extensive and elaborate explanations. The choirmaster should make his choir feel that they are his associates. Their work should be made educative, so that they become discerning and intelligent co-workers. Even when a choir has become quite competent, the choirmaster will always find new problems constantly arising, interesting alike to himself and to his singers.

THERE ARE many ways of making rehearsals interesting and attractive. As has been said, the music practiced at a rehearsal will naturally be of varied character. Some will be vigorous and energetic, some quiet and sustained. An effective alternation adds greatly to the life of a rehearsal. Loud, vigorous music should not be practiced so long as to cause fatigue; neither should quiet music be allowed to induce heaviness and lack of animation. Each may be used to relieve the other. Each may heighten the pleasure of the other. Then too, vitality may be secured by taking up some fairly short compositions after practice on an extended one. The span will be different. Moreover, the shorter ones, being naturally more concentrated in character, will vary the type of attention involved. Though alternation of characteristically loud music and soft music and of compositions of distinctly different dimensions and character may be very serviceable, it must be discreetly employed. Jumping from this to that—helter-skelter rehearsing—is tiring and irksome.

Another enlivening form of variety available in rehearsing is to be found in the different sorts of work which are necessary in the preparation of choir music: roughing-in and polishing. On the one hand, there is note-learning and other elementary work to be done; and on the other hand, expression and interpretation to be gained. Note-learning and other spade work should be done with little regard to expression except to that of the general style of the composition, as *sostenuto* or *animato*. Accuracy in notes and time values must be insisted on, but unnecessary "spelling out" should be avoided. In taking up a new composition it is generally wise to run it through, either in its entirety, or section by section in case it is an extended anthem, in order that the choir may get the feel of the music. In doing this twice or possibly three times many wrong notes will have corrected themselves and the rhythmic and structural features as well as the spirit of the music be perceived by the singers. Roughing-in should have place in the middle of the rehearsal, not too near the beginning or the end; it should be resorted to rather abruptly, as a novelty introducing fresh music, but it ought not to be carried on for too long a time.

By roughing-in some music and refining other a greater amount of music will be practiced at each rehearsal than would otherwise be the case, and not only will there be variety in the sort of work done, but each phase of the preparation will receive more careful consideration. The rehearsal will be more thorough-going. Worthy music will receive adequate practice, and through successive rehearsals over a period of two, three or more weeks it will have time to sink in—an important consideration, for the best music is not assimilated at sight, it must be lived with.

To gain accuracy and assurance in the individual parts and to attain an excellent body and effective balance of tone it is often well to practice two or three voice parts together. Generally speaking, the lower parts should receive more attention than they are usually given. It is in the inner parts that wrong notes most frequently occur. Moreover, *crescendos* in church music are best made by comparatively large *crescendos* in the lower parts; these, surging up as a mass, support the highest voices, relieving them of undue effort. The welling up of the lower voices allows the highest voice to float on top. By this treatment of the voice parts it is possible to secure a sense of fulness, largeness and climax without straining and stridency. Especially in unaccompanied singing dynamic contrasts are readily and effectively attained by comparatively greater variations in the lower than in the upper parts.

In order to stabilize a lower part it is frequently desirable, if the passage admits, to have the tenors and basses unite in singing a tenor or bass passage which offers difficulties either as to notes or rhythm. The same is true with regard to the upper parts. Such part-rehearsing stimulates and concentrates the attention of those engaged in it, but it must not be continued too long with any one set. In contrapuntal music the practicing of two parts together, and then perhaps three, gives sureness, while in harmonic music, building up from the bass, adding first the tenor, then the alto and finally the soprano, induces that firmness and sustained character which is most desirable in church music.

The tonal beauty of the several parts in a chorus is largely dependent upon the director. He has, of course, to work with the given material, and generally there will be some flecks in it, but he must make the most of what he has. He should seek to blend each voice part, fusing all the voices on it into a single strand of unified tone. No one voice should stand out from the others. This is a matter for the director to have constantly in mind and also for the members of the group to co-operate in attaining.

Then there is the matter of balance of parts. In general, all the parts of chords should be alike in volume. Not infrequently this is not attained because voices are not of uniform volume and of the same quality throughout their range. Upper notes are naturally stronger and stand out more. As all the notes of a chord are not always in the same general region of their respective vocal registers, it is necessary to guard against inequality. If, for instance, the bass is in its highest register and the others are in their lower registers, the volume and prominence of the bass should be reduced to correspond with that of the other voices. In making such adjustments the various voices should be scaled to the weakest part. And again, the dispersion of the voice parts in chords should be taken into consideration. When the component notes of a chord are not fairly equidistant, care must be taken to make them into an harmonic unit. It should not be felt in a four-part chord, for instance, that there are three notes in a group here and one note there. The several parts must be unified. When the bass part is a tenth below the tenor, the spread should be covered by having the bass somewhat stronger than it would otherwise be,

181

or if a soprano—especially in the highest register—is an octave away from the alto, the alto and the voices below it should be made sufficiently strong to keep the soprano from being felt to be isolated. In the case of wide stretches between voices, the strengthening of the lower part or parts will do away with the gap.

In choral music all the notes of a chord are not always equally important. There are often salient notes which, if properly treated, give distinctive expressiveness and added fulness. These telling notes are generally in the middle parts of the harmony—the thirds, fifths and sevenths. They are particularly important in widely-spaced chords and especially so when the outer voice duplicates the fundamental of the chord. This harmonic aspect of choral singing is a subtle and fascinating art. It is a matter which, unfortunately, is seldom adequately attended to by choir directors. It should, in fact, be understood and cared for not only by the director but by the singers as well, for they are active partners; the more intelligent co-workers are, the better will be the results. Not all singers or directors realize that the loudest chord is not necessarily the most sonorous, and that in church music it is generally fulness and firmness rather than mere loudness that is to be sought in *forte* passages.

Entrances of separate voice parts in contrapuntal music, and in harmonic music as well, should be clearly effected; but after a voice has asserted itself, it should yield, imperceptibly, to other entrants. It should not, however, fade away. There should be a give-and-take in contrapuntal passages, each part, however, maintaining its integrity. When, in comparatively quiet music, a section or phrase begins with a single voice part, care should be taken that the body of tone employed is sufficiently strong; for, being heard alone, it is likely, unless it is in the bass part, to sound feeble and timid.

Moving parts which are significant melodically, rhythmically, or harmonically should be given their due prominence. Counterpoising these moving parts in the musical structure are commonly other parts which move but little, if at all. Now these more static parts are very likely to protrude, for one naturally sings sustained or repeated notes and those which are but little varied with greater surety and strength than those which are moving. They are consequently liable to eclipse active and characteristically expressive parts. Persistently repeated or sustained tones, used as harmonic background and filling, should not be allowed to blanket interesting and vitalizing parts. The poorer composers are addicted to writing many stationary notes, and it is the poorer choirs who stress such notes in performance.

In ensemble music the singers' power of listening is important and should be cultivated. All the voices on a part should be completely fused and each part be well-proportioned in the ensemble. In bringing this about, the choir singer is, with composer and conductor, a creative artist in church music.

It is highly desirable for the singer to have an understanding of the structure of the music he sings, its general form and its repeated and related phrases and sections. Good music is logical; art is coherent. Vitally to realize this is very important. The education of the choir in this matter, increasing their intelligence and competency, is a concern for the director. This he may effect through critical comments on the music in hand. These must be brief and really enlightening and are best made incidentally. In every instance they should be specific, relating this phrase with that, this section with that, noting similarities and significant dissimilarities and pointing out their structural and expressional purpose. Sugary or weak music does not respond to such treatment, while music which is strong and worthy becomes more meaningful. Through perception of its general structure and understanding of its significant details the best music will be more readily learned in the rehearsal room and more effectively performed in the service.

Phrasing, musical and verbal, is a matter of importance. Many choir singers are merely note- and syllable-singers with the result that there is little or no musical or verbal sense in what they do. Their singing is dull and without significance.

Often they themselves feel this to be so and attempt to improve it and secure animation through increased speed and volume—generally the two in combination. But if we are to have expression in vocal music syllables, words and notes are not to be uniformly stressed.

In many instances choir music is dull because instead of its having a rhythmical vitality there is metrical plodding. All the beats in a measure are pretty much alike; first beats, if they are observed at all, are regularly pounded out. There is neither expression nor beauty. Instead of forcing the tone on the accented beats it is well to lighten up on the weaker beats, as we do in speech. As a result there will be freedom and flow, ease and grace—stability as well. The secondary beats will, so to speak, be stepping stones, rather than stopping places: the music will gain in movement and in breadth. Moreover, by making the secondary beats lighter, rather than the accented beats stronger, the level of loudness will be lower, which in many cases would be most agreeable, for choir music is often needlessly and uniformly too loud. There should be animation, but never blatancy.

It is often advisable to rehearse a composition at a different pace from that determined for its performance. Sometimes the tempo chosen may be slower, sometimes faster than the intended pace—slower for gaining security and sonority, faster for gaining animation and vital breadth of rhythm. In certain instances it may be well at rehearsal to exaggerate nuances in order to impress them on the minds of the singers so that they will surely be given their right value at performance.

Expression in choir music should as much as possible be effected vocally. Organists ought not to coach their choirs during the service. Not infrequently they tend in the service to overproduce on the organ the expression which they have sought to have the choir give to the music, more or less unconsciously carrying over from the rehearsal their efforts to induce the choir to attain this.

Marks of expression should be so interpreted as to give life and meaning to the music and not be merely mechanically rendered. Expression in choir music should be felt as expression of religious thought and mood, and not as a distinct and obvious musical feature. On account of its character and purpose, there is properly less marked variation in dynamics in church music than in secular music. Choir music should not, however, be all *mezzo forte*. While there should be dynamic contrasts, these ought not to be startling or artificial. There should be refinement in nuance, but refinement should not be pursued to such an extent as to become mere finesse. Everything should be done for the purpose of deepening the religious mood, not as a display of musical accomplishment.

Piano and *forte* are relative terms artistically, not absolute quantities. A *forte* should always be solid and substantial and have a certain vigor, but it should be realized that a large volume of tone if it comes after an interval of silence or after a *pianissimo* passage sounds much greater and much more forceful than the same body of tone succeeding a *piano* passage. Against a background of silence it comes as a thrust. Violent, startling outbursts are out of place in sacred music. Sometimes, however, the choir may quite properly rise suddenly to a big climax, as is called for in many settings of the passage in the *Te Deum*, "To Thee Cherubim and Seraphim continually do cry, Holy, Holy, Holy, Lord God of Sabaoth." In this matter of dynamic expression choir directors are frequently at fault, mechanically obeying the marks in the score, but failing to gain their expressive intention.

As has been said, quality of tone is important. Some directors carefully develop the vocal character of their choirs, while others are content merely to suppress what is disagreeable, or neglect the matter entirely. Though every director has of course to work with a given material, he should seek to improve it vocally. But is the choir director competent to undertake such improvement? And will the members of the choir submit to such training as is necessary? As to the first of these questions, it should be said that a choir director ought to make himself familiar with at least the rudiments and know common faults in singing and the means of their correction. As to the second, he will find the choir willing to do vocal training, provided he is competent and if the matter is discreetly introduced. Generally the vocal building up of a choir is best begun incidentally, through attention to enunciation or to sustained and accurate vowel singing. The choir will immediately see the pertinency of this, after which more extensive and regular attention to this matter will be felt to be desirable. For instance, a beautiful sustained volume of tone, both *forte* and *piano*, may be obtained by having the choir hum or vocalize, first on "loo," the successive notes of a tune such as *Nun Danket*, seeing to it that each note is extended to its full length. Later, words should be sung, consonants being tacked on, "fore and aft," as they occur, while care is taken that these do not affect the sustaining of the various vowels.

In sacred music the tone should in general be of a *sostenuto* character. Music which has notes the singers cannot reach without obviously great effort ought to be avoided. Composers, it should be said, could in many instances write music which would be more commonly available and effective by having greater regard to this matter of range. Music with high notes, especially when these are isolated and far removed from the lower parts, is generally undesirable in that such notes are liable to give a sensational and secular feeling to the music. Choir music need not be mellifluous, but it should be agreeable.

Careful attention ought also to be given to the words. How the composer studies them! They are the inspiring source of the musical setting. The music augments the inherent character and expressiveness of the text. As the words are a source of inspiration for the composer, so they should be also for the performer. If at rehearsal their meaning and musical expression are apparently not grasped by the choir, phrases or sections should be read aloud by the director, not formally, but incidentally as the foundation for the musical expression—which they are. With a more complete perception of the lofty spirit of the text, the glory of church music will be more fully attained. A sensitive understanding of the words will not only stimulate the attention and interest but also impart character to the interpretation and inspiration to the performance of the music.

From time to time it is well for the director to leave the chancel or organ loft and listen to his choir from the body of the church. This he may do at a regular Sunday morning rehearsal in the church or at a week night rehearsal. Occasionally it is desirable to conduct the first part of the rehearsal in the choir room and the latter part in the church. Listening to one's choir from the body of the church enables the director to discover many things and to learn much. He will find some things better than he anticipated and others not so good. In attempting to gauge the volume of tone of his choir he should bear in mind that in an empty church there is more resonance than when a congregation is present. Clothes absorb sound.

Wherever possible a piano should be the instrument used at rehearsal. The organ is undesirable in that it covers up faults. A grand piano is best, not because of its size—a small grand is as good for the purpose as a concert grand—but because the singers may be grouped about it in such a way that the director may best control attention, give direction and work with concentration and efficiency. Unaccompanied practice ought to be resorted to much more than it commonly is. The choir should be trained to be vocally substantial and self-reliant, for choir music is fundamentally vocal music. The piano in the choir room, if it is to be helpful and not harmful, must, of course, be in tune.

During actual work the closest attention should be insisted on. Yet, while rehearsals should be conducted at high tension, means should be taken not to overtire the choir and allow the work to become irritating or boresome. As has been pointed out, this may be variously done: through change of music practiced, through alternation of loud vigorous music with that which is quiet and sustained, and through change in the kind of work. If the rehearsal is very long, it may be well to have a five-minute intermission in the middle, but after it the director must be sure to bring the members back to full attention immediately.

ON SUNDAYS the choirmaster should be on hand early and see that everything is in readiness, the copies of music orderly arranged and all preliminaries, even the smallest, attended to. Everything in the church should be fully prepared at least fifteen minutes before the service. During these fifteen minutes there should be no conversation, no unnecessary movements about the church. Except for suitable organ music in preparation for the service, there should be silence in the church—it ought to be generally understood that silence and reverence are befitting the sanctuary.

The members of the choir should not be permitted to straggle in or wander about the choir loft or stalls. The choir most properly enters as a body, their entrance denoting the beginning of the service. The service should start promptly at the appointed time, everything clearly having been prepared, minister, choirs, ushers and sexton performing their respective functions with unanimity and perfect understanding.

During the service the choir, being generally in an exceptionally conspicuous place, has to maintain a degree of decorum not requisite even for those in the pews. They are so prominently before the eyes of everybody that the slightest movement— turning the head, to say nothing of conversing, finding music, turning pages—is noticeable and detracting. Arrangements ought to be such that movements by the choir before and during the service are as inconsiderable as possible. Care should be taken to secure simultaneous rising and sitting of the choral body, which should be practiced until they have become almost automatic. Then too, music should not be folded up until the anthem is ended and the choir is ready to be seated. The choirmaster should be responsible for the conduct of the choir. It would seem unnecessary to speak of reverence and behavior during the service, but unfortunately those of all ages are sometimes remiss in this matter.

As far as possible the choir should participate in all the parts of the service, not only in those with which they are especially charged but also in the responsive reading, in corporate prayers and in responses. The choirmaster and minister may tactfully establish this as a general custom. The sense of continuity and of earnest purposiveness and wholeheartedness in the service may be greatly augmented by the choir. Those in the pews realize this probably more than the choir does. It is an assistance which should not be withheld.

The spacing of the component parts of the service is a matter which needs to be carefully considered by those conducting it. Too sudden or too detached successions are to be avoided. There is art—which is both expressive and impressive—in the way the parts of a religious service should properly succeed each other. The ceremonial rhythm and inflection of a service is an integral and vital part of it. Both formally and emotionally the parts should be well-articulated; the service should flow along naturally and freely. The parts ought not to succeed each other hurriedly, breathlessly, creating the feeling that the service is being rammed through; nor on the other hand, should their succession be hesitating or languid. The time interstices should be neither too long nor too short. Frequently there is a too sudden taking up of one's part. The organist jumps in the instant a hymn or a collection is announced, startling those in the pews and causing them to feel that he has been impatiently waiting for his turn and is a little unceremonious in taking it; or again, the minister in the responsive readings treads upon the heels of the congregation or begins to announce his text before the organ has fully ceased. The opposite of this, of course—gaps and halting successions—is also undesirable. Those in charge should realize that by appropriately spacing the successive parts of a service they may greatly affect its character and enhance its value. But if this is to be attained, spacing must be inherently expressive, not something superficial.

Breaks in the proceedings of the period of worship are definitely planned by some churches to allow for the seating of late-comers. Pauses are indicated on the program during which "the ushers will seat those who may be waiting." Several gaps, in fact, are sometimes left for this purpose. On a calendar before me the places in the order of service for the entrance of late-comers are triple-starred—should they not rather be triple daggered! Devotionally, the period for seating is a dead spot; it detracts from the spirit of worship. Why should it be assumed that the congregation is not assembled at the time of the beginning of the service? Why should late-comers be given a status? Why is provision made and propriety extended to those who are from five to fifteen minutes late? Tardiness is largely a matter of habit. It is a bad habit, and ought not to be encouraged by being given amiable recognition. Why may not late-comers be disposed of by having them take seats in the rear which might be reserved for them? Why parade them up to seats in the front? The less prominence and favor given to late-comers the better. Halts and waits in the service are defects; they are not conducive to worship, but quite the reverse. And during these intervals in the service the organist plays aimlessly, merely to fill in the time and try to cover over the gap.

THE DIRECTOR should possess sufficient musical ability and competency in directing to have the confidence and respect of the members of the choir and the congregation. Alert, tactful, never fretful or peevish, serious and intent, he should have, together with endless patience, an unlimited store of enthusiasm. All the members of his choir should be known by him individually, none should be anonymous; and he should treat them as human beings and not as so many organ pipes. He should be cordial to all, with a little personal reserve, but yet not aloof or offish. The personality of the director and his discretion in conducting affairs are extremely important in making the choir attractive and successful.

A large proportion of those in the choir are there not from a single interest, religious, musical, or social. With most members the musical interest is the strongest. This is natural. Musical excellence is, indeed, very desirable in choir work, and may well be magnified—and this can be done without expense to the religious. The attractiveness of choir membership depends very largely upon whether the choir sings well—so also does the quality of service the choir can render the church. For a chorus to be really successful, its work must be substantial and good. This means that there must be adequate, intelligent rehearsing. The preparation of music for the service should be so thorough that there is no fear or uncertainty on the part of the singers. Then, and then only, can the singers sing with freedom and spontaneity and enter fully into the spirit of the service. In this connection it should not be overlooked that inadequate performance naturally tends to cause the congregation to hold the choir and choir music in comparatively little musical and devotional esteem.

The social side of choir life should receive due attention. Frequently it does not. The director should know all the members of his choir individually and members should know one another. Nothing so stimulates loyalty to a group as the realization that one is an actual and definite part of it. In many instances members of a choir, besides being religious co-workers and musical associates, become fast friends. The bond of friendship is a unifying and stabilizing force. In most chorus choirs there should be opportunity for social intercourse. A distinctly social period at the close of the regular rehearsal once a month with light refreshments served will be of benefit to choir morale.

Although the choirmaster and choir members may do much to promote the social life of the choir, others may aid in doing this. The church, for instance, may appropriate a small sum to provide refreshments for social meetings of the choir. Those who regularly give their services to the church work should sometimes be invited guests at church suppers. On such occasions the choir should be genuine guests, and not always, like "Little Tommy Tucker," have to "sing for their supper." Again, social meetings of the choir now and then at the home of the chairman of the music committee or members of it, or at the parsonage, will do much to stimulate and improve choir spirit.

Though the musical and social elements in choir life should be cared for, a religious character must never be lacking in church music. Some members of the choir may be deeply imbued with the religious functioning of church music, but it will devolve upon the director to ensure the presence of the religious element. It may be effected through the materials he selects, both words and music, through the interpretation of these and the spirit of performance he inculcates in the choir, and through his manner and spirit in both the rehearsal and the service. It is important that there be a right atmosphere. Neither in the rehearsal nor in the service should the choir sing, as they often do, as if they were doing penance. There should be brightness and joy, but always a due sense of reverence. While there should in general be a tone of seriousness in the rehearsal, pertinent alike to the character of the music and the attainment of musical excellence, a hearty laugh now and then may be most desirable. But witty or humorous remarks ought never be made during the rehearsal of solemn music. The choirmaster should ever have before him the sublime religious function of church music. This should be felt and transmitted to the choir, but not dilated upon. Unobtrusively the choirmaster should, naturally and instinctively, create the requisite religious atmosphere in his choir.

In securing a religious quality in the music of the church and also in establishing and maintaining a high morale in the choir the minister may greatly assist the choirmaster. Often, at least in the eyes of the choir, minister and choirmaster are not co-workers; they do business on the same street, but they are not partners. Choirmasters are as a rule almost always ready, openly and cordially to recognize the minister as head of the firm, if he is willing to form one with them. Very often, though the most cordial personal relation exists between choirmaster and minister, there is little or no co-operation between them. As the minister is the superior officer, it is of course his place to initiate such co-operation.

The choir rehearsal should not be a thing entirely foreign

to the minister. A visit now and then to the rehearsal, at which he may possibly make some brief illuminating comments about church music in general or in detail or about the service, will help considerably in establishing the sense of the high function of the church service and of church music in it. He should, however, as a general thing, not remain at the rehearsal long. Neither in the choir room nor in the pulpit should he patronize the choir. The minister best shows his appreciation of the choir and exercises his highest influence on them by conducting the service in such a manner that their portion becomes an integral and vital part of it. He should always recognize the director as the head of the choir, as superintendent of that department. By his action and attitude he may increase the regard in which the director is held by the choir and also elevate the status of the choir in the estimation of its members and heighten their loyalty and support. Much of the success of a choir may sometimes be traced to the minister.

THE SELECTING of the musical parts of the service—in nonliturgical churches this means both words and music—is one of the director's most important duties. His choice as to words may be made with reference to the general structure of the service or in conference with the minister. In services of nonconformist churches it is well to have two anthems. The first should generally be of comparatively large dimensions, broad and majestic in style, the music having dignity and sweep, the words being religiously objective; the second should be of somewhat smaller dimensions, less active and more reflective, an anthem of more particular reference and of more intimate sentiment. Coming, as they properly should, in the two characteristic sections of the period of worship, each in accord with the particular devotional mood and character of the section in which it occurs, they should be potent means of rendering the service more worthy and exalting. Such diversity obviates monotony and secures dynamic integration of the several vital elements in religious worship.

The problem of new music is constantly before the director. To sing anthems over and over demoralizes the choir and either stupefies or irritates the congregation. Choirs, on their part, need incentive and challenge. They need new music to stir their interest and new tasks to increase their efficiency; but these should not be beyond their capabilities. The director must also consider the receptivity of the congregation. Too much unfamiliar music is both unwelcome and ineffective. The best church music does not disclose its full beauty and expressiveness at a single hearing. Music of value and distinction merits being heard more than once; in fact, it often needs several hearings, especially if it is rather elaborate or is written in a comparatively new idiom or style. In introducing anthems of a new type or those employing an unfamiliar idiom, the director should choose pieces which are not over-complicated or over-long. By being comparatively simple and short, they will be better prepared and presented by the choir and also better received by the congregation. Such music should be more than casually used; it should be so placed in the service that the congregation may enter into its spirit and find themselves in its expressiveness. Some directors overestimate the assimilative powers of their congregation or seem to disregard the matter.

Music which is to be repeated—and almost all the choir music in a service is music which has been sung before—should always be rehearsed with renewed and fresh emphasis on phrasing, dynamics and expression. And not only should anthems be rejuvenated, the more constant parts of the service, the chants and responses, should also be kept animated. The latter are often overlooked, and as a consequence become dull and perfunctory. Every now and then it is wise to make them a special item for consideration, studying out before rehearsal just how they may be improved and brought to the point of their greatest expressiveness. Too often they are only casually run over in the chancel just before the service. In many churches they seem to go a long time wholly neglected.

THE DIRECTOR

Choir directors often find two groups in their churches, who may be designated as "the louds" and "the softs," those whose devotional mood and feeling is jubilant, buoyant and militant and those who are of a more reflective nature, whose devotional mood is meditative, quiet and reserved. The former desire bright, energetic music, while the latter prefer music of a subdued and reposeful order. Individual churches are likely to be distinctly more of one type than the other. A wide disparity between the devotional mood of the congregation and that of the director is very unfortunate, causing the music, however good in its performance, to be unsatisfactory.

Directors should not be insensible to the fact that within the congregations they serve there will be those of both temperaments, each of which should be given due recognition. Worship properly has two quite different moods, one comparatively active and exultant, the other quietly introspective, sensitive, and restrained. How these moods shall be apportioned and related is a problem to engage his careful attention. This whole matter, therefore, of "the louds" and "the softs," considered broadly, pertains not merely to the director's getting on with his employers—the music committee, the minister and the congregation—but has also to do with his being inherently efficient in the work committed to his charge.

THE RELATIVE AMOUNT of music to be practiced at a rehearsal and that to be used in the service is a matter to be carefully considered by the director. At the rehearsal it is desirable to take up quantitatively as much music as can be rehearsed profitably, using various means and methods of rehearsing in gaining efficiency. On the other hand, there should not be, as there sometimes is, too much choir music in the service. Variety of type of music and excellence of performance, coupled with effective placement of the choir numbers in relation to the other parts, should be given more attention than they usually receive.

Choir directors are frequently at fault in being too ambitious

195

in their planning and not sufficiently exacting in the preparation of their music. It is, of course, difficult to estimate unerringly the potentialities of a situation, but a director should not inflict on a complacent congregation music which is inadequately prepared.

The best choirs aim less at elaboration than at perfection. One of the great indiscretions in our church music, however, is that of the choir's attempting works beyond their capabilities and public performance of music which they have not mastered. Many choirs and directors apparently think that it is sufficient if they manage to get through their music without collapse. Now every good musician realizes how essential adequate performance is. It is a great misfortune that the best music is often not rightly presented. Excellence of composition is not everything—neither is the composer's name; excellence of performance is requisite. Every composer is at the mercy of the performer—and so is every audience and every congregation. Small wonder is it that many people do not like "classical music," secular or sacred — for they may never really have heard it.

All music used in a service ought to have been thoroughly prepared at rehearsal. Not infrequently musical compositions which we hear in church should have been kept longer in the workshop, the choir room. Scratch performance in church is inexcusable. The choirmaster, it is true, may not have had time enough with his choir to attain the desired result—exceptionally he may be the victim of circumstances; but it is one of the requisites of a good conductor to be able to cut his coat according to the cloth.

Inadequacy of performance is not, however, always occasioned by lack of opportunity for sufficient practice. In many instances it is due to the choirmaster's lack of ability to conceive an ideal performance of the music in hand and to his lack of technical understanding and skill for attaining it. Poor performance is often due to his inability to see how much better it could be. Instead of perfecting the music in hand, the director undertakes new music; note-reading is engaged in, and the matter of interpretation and of otherwise attaining really effective performance is given comparatively little attention.

It is important that the choirmaster have a clear perception of the function of church music and understand the means of gaining expressiveness in choral sacred music. It is possible for him to heed every gradation mark and yet fail to grasp and impart the inner meaning of the music. The latent expressiveness of the best church music is not always revealed; one director may make glorious and sublime what in the hands of another is dull and lifeless.

The choir should be made aware of the beauty and expressiveness of the music they sing. This the director does best, not by expatiating on the subject, but by bringing out the innate excellence of the music through his interpretation of it. By intelligently working on phrasing, nuance, balance of parts, tempo and style, he may bring his choir to a realization of the significance and worth of the music in hand. This will be stimulating, beneficial to the work of the choir and helpful in maintaining a high morale. Then choir work will be rewarding, musically and religiously, and not be engaged in with that slack condescension with which it is often treated.

ALTHOUGH the director has much influence on church music, he does not by any means have full and exclusive control. He is not monarch of all he surveys. Far from it. His position is delicate, subtle, and more or less unstable. It is peculiar in that at once he is at the mercy of those whom he serves, and they in turn are at his mercy and are influenced by him. He is judged by their standards, not by his own; but he is in a position, if he is retained for a sufficient period in the service of the given church, to modify to a degree their ideals and their standards of judgment. The choirmaster is generally confronted with conditions not wholly to his liking, but he has his opportunity to change and improve them. Through his conduct of affairs he is constantly confirming or transforming present practice.

The congregation has a collective standard of taste by which things are judged, but this standard owes its inception to an individual.

The organist and director is not infrequently confronted with the problem as to how far he can go in meeting the wishes of the committee who hires him and yet maintain his religious and artistic conscience. The true church musician has an ideal and is not a mere hireling. But he must recognize what is practical musically in his particular position and what is possible receptively on the part of the congregation. We must meet people where we find them—but it is not necessary or honest to remain there. A leader in church music must be in touch with those whom he leads. He should make himself at home with their point of view, but he should ever strive to raise the character of church music and elevate its function. In doing this he should at once be conscientious and reasonable.

However carefully a director may plan and arrange things, contingencies will every now and then arise which necessitate immediate change. "The best laid schemes o' mice and men gang aft a-gley." Singers are out of voice; absences may deplete a section of the choir; members may be present at rehearsal or service, but not at both; epidemics of colds for weeks affect the work of a choir. Then there are severe storms which interfere with attendance; and now and then certain social or musical events of great or general interest practically necessitate change or omission of the rehearsal. Such things block a director's plans; but he must always make the best of even a bad situation, either by changing plans or by pushing ahead with the listed music as best he can. An emergency anthem, one for general use, comparatively simple and familiar to the choir, ought always to be available. Whatever incidental solos there may be in them should be practiced so as to be familiar to all singing the part: then, in case the intended soloist is absent or incapacitated, another can be designated at the moment, or better perhaps, the entire section be called into requisition. The congregation know nothing of these difficulties. They only know, possibly, that the music is not according to announcement or is not as extensive as usual. The director may be criticized because excellence is not attained under trying and perhaps impossible conditions—but these things are incidental to his work and position.

CHOIR EFFICIENCY is something which has to be constantly maintained. It is, so to speak, like a boulder poised on a side of a hill, having to be kept from sliding down by the giant hand of the choirmaster. It is an error to suppose that excellence of a choir can be retained without effort. Director and choir must labor unceasingly. Always to make each occasion the momentous occasion is the secret of long pre-eminence in efficiency. It is comparatively easy to push up the hill — enthusiasm, novelty, and zest in overcoming obstacles contribute to the effort —but when these incentives and impulses have been used up, then the real test comes. Many choirs having made an excellent attainment begin to rest on it, relaxing the insistent and repeated practice by which the original success was obtained. To go over old material with the ardor of the first attempt tests one's tenacity of purpose and ideal. Inexperienced singers, it should be said, are sometimes more desirable than those who do not feel that they are in need of any considerable practice; those who have sung many years in the choir do not always realize that greater distinction lies ahead, and that it has ever to be won. Maintenance of excellence is to be had only through an unremitting insistence on the present task. The choir which begins to curtail its rehearsals and run on its own momentum is running downhill. Trusting to past attainment and to the inspiration of the moment are twin failings—conceit and indifference — though they may not be recognized as such. Choirmaster and choir have ever to be alert and efficient in the task committed to their charge.

To bear, as the true church musician does, the chalice of the people's devotions in his hands is indeed a high and sacred office.

199

CHAPTER XIV

THE ORGANIST

WHETHER the organist is also director of the choir or not, his influence in the service is very great. He has to do with the congregation in the hymns, with the choir in the anthems and chants, and he makes his own purely instrumental contribution in the prelude and postlude and mediating interludes, and, it may be, also in the offertory. His influence permeates the service, enhancing its musical parts or rendering them vapid. More than anyone else the organist shares with the minister the responsibility for the religious atmosphere of the service. His is a major position among church musicians.

On the organ bench in our churches are to be found persons of quite diverse musical capabilities, varying from those who have been drafted into service—not because they are competent but because they can play even a little, as is frequently the case in very small churches and in remote rural districts—to those in the largest and most well-to-do churches who are professional and sometimes concert organists. Except in rare cases the vocation of organist is a side profession. For the most part church organists are either persons engaged in business or professional pursuits who devote some of their spare time to church music, or persons engaged in teaching piano, voice or public school music, for whom organ music and organ playing is more or less of an incidental interest and activity. If we exclude concert organists and the very few organists who have daily services, the distinction between professional and amateur organists is not always so important as it might appear at first sight, for both classes generally act as organists only on Sundays. The professional musician—the one who earns his livelihood

200

wholly in music—will probably have the superior technical equipment, though this may not always be the case. Among the so-called amateur organists are many men and women of superior musical education and proficiency, whose generous service is a great asset to the church.

The dearth of really satisfactory organists in many communities is due in large measure to an all too common short-sighted and narrow-minded policy on the part of churches towards those who wish to study and perfect themselves in organ-playing. It is often very difficult for students wishing to study under capable teachers to secure the necessary facilities for practice. How are they to make themselves competent to serve the church? How practice without an organ? At best, the organ student can ordinarily practice hardly during more than half of the year, since daily practice in most churches is out of the question in the cold months. Instead of denying him the means of perfecting himself, even if he is not to be appointed organist of the particular church, a policy of generosity and assistance, with privileges duly safeguarded, should be adopted for serious students desiring to make themselves capable of rendering service to the church as organists.

The organ as an instrument makes requisitions on the organist which are in a number of ways quite different from those made on the pianist. Unlike pianos, organs differ very much in their construction and general make-up. They vary interminably in details. Effective organ playing requires not only manual and pedal facility but also much ingenuity and adaptation in the handling of a particular instrument. The organ-builder does much towards making effective organ music possible by providing an instrument the softer stops of which have a beautiful and individually distinctive quality of tone and its louder stops an imposing and majestic character. It is, however, for the organist to use this palette of delicate color and this stately body of tone for expressive purpose in the church service. To do this well a fine sense of tone quality and balance is requisite both for music which is soft and quiet and also for that which is vigorous and loud. As has been said of the traveler that he brings back from foreign lands that which he took with him, so the organist brings forth from his instrument what is existent in his musical sense and imagination. Organ playing is distinctly musically creative in character.

The office of organist is one requiring very considerable general musical intelligence and knowledge. More than any other class of musicians the organist needs a practical knowledge of harmony, counterpoint and musical form; then too, having to work with various individuals and musical bodies—the congregation, the minister, the choir and perhaps soloists—he needs discretion and tact in dealing, both musically and personally, with individuals and with groups.

In addition to these qualifications, the church organist should have a genuine devotional sense. It is the possession of this in his work which differentiates him as a church organist. It is a faculty which requires cultivation and upon which much of the success of his work will depend. Unfortunately, little or no provision is usually made in the organist's education for this part of his equipment. A great advance will be made when facilities are provided for meeting this desideratum, and organists are adequately prepared not only in the musical but in the liturgical and devotional phases of their work.

IN SELECTING an organist, churches frequently make the mistake of basing their choice too much on the qualifications of the candidate as a solo player; the performance of specially prepared pieces is often given undue emphasis. As a matter of fact, the church organist has comparatively little solo work to do in the service. His efficiency in the position is found rather in his capabilities in congregational leadership, in choir accompaniment, and in linking together the various parts of the service.

A satisfactory solo player may be very mediocre as a church organist, while one who is not proficient in recital work may be very successful. The type of music and style of performance appropriate in concert and recital playing are quite different from those in a religious service. Mere virtuosity is not only uncalled for in the church service—it is out of place. An elaborate and brilliant organ composition after the service may be grateful to some of the congregation, but it should not be in the body of the service or too closely appended to it. More important than brilliant keyboard technique in a church organist is broad musical intelligence, religious feeling, and practical adaptiveness. This is not to say that a good technique is not desirable—the more ample it is the better—but it must be used for the purpose of the church and not for display.

IN THE COURSE of the service the organist generally acts in three capacities: as organist pure and simple, chiefly in the prelude and postlude; as leader of the congregation in the hymns; and as accompanist of the choir in the chants and anthems. Each of these roles is distinctive. In an earlier chapter we have spoken of the organist in the purely instrumental music of the service. It remains for us to consider him here as leader in congregational music and as accompanist of the choir.

Playing for congregational singing is presumably the simplest work the organist has to do. Yet it is seldom accomplished as well as it might be; not infrequently it is done in a perfunctory way. In leading and supporting hymn singing, of which with the exception of the *Gloria Patri* congregational music consists, there are two matters which call for special attention: the playing-over of the tune and the playing with the singing. Each of these has its own problems.

The playing-over of the tune should constitute an inspiring pattern leading up to the singing. The tempo should be that in which the hymn is to be sung and the volume and quality of tone such as to indicate its spirit. Just what the tempo and volume of tone should be in a given instance depends upon several things—the character and mood of the hymn and the tune, the size of the building and of the congregation, and the mood of the particular place in the service at which the hymn is introduced.

Many organists are deplorably indecisive and unsteady in giving out a tune. They do not definitely realize the appropriate tempo before beginning to play, but feel about for it as they play, falling into several tempos in the meantime. This is the unskilled amateur's way. The competent musician realizes that the secondary beats in the first full measure should establish the tempo of the composition; he does not grope about to find his way and get the pace. His artistic sense of proprieties projects it. The tempo and rhythm in the playing-over of the tune should be definite and clear-cut, so broad and convincing that when the congregation begin to sing, they will do so with confidence and assurance.

Invariably to announce tunes with a stereotyped combination of stops, as many organists do, is a dull procedure. The same volume and character of tone is not equally suited to all hymns, for hymns are not all alike in mood. Many organists have the habit of regularly playing the tune over on the swell organ. Where the organ is large this may be effective, but in many churches the playing-over of the tune on the swell organ sounds weak and puny, a mere cue. Then again, some organists are prone to "solo the melody." This has its risks; it may make the melody prominent, but tempo and rhythm are likely to suffer. Generally speaking, congregational tunes should be frankly presented in a broad way, for congregational singing is mass singing. The preliminary playing should set the tempo and suggest the general volume and character of tone which is to be used in the first stanza. Pedals, it should be said, are not necessary and in general should not be used in giving out a tune. Their entrance in the first stanza gives impetus to the singing of the congregation.

In some quarters the practice of playing over the entire tune is felt to be superfluous and irritating and the complete playing-over is dispensed with. Four or eight measures, ending with a full cadence, are made to establish the tempo, mood and general character of the tune. Tunes of double metre, it should be noted, may be more readily and effectively abbreviated than others. But if the playing-over is abbreviated, it should not be a mangled, indefinite affair; furthermore, there should be a definite understanding with the minister and choir in this matter so that they may rise sufficiently early for the singing and the congregation not be taken by surprise and fail to be in readiness to sing at the beginning of the hymn.

IN LEADING and accompanying congregational singing, the organist should use a substantial body of tone. While this may not always be of the same volume, it should never be so soft as to seem timid or so loud as to be coarse and boisterous. He should give the congregation adequate support so that the feeling of isolation which makes them afraid to lift up their voices may be prevented; at the same time the organist should be careful lest he override the voices. He should seek to develop vitality in the congregation rather than play to carry along their dead weight. A *forte* accompaniment, with steadiness and breadth of phrasing, is better than *fortissimo* playing. A graduated *fortissimo,* momentarily flooding the church with tone, may occasionally be desirable, but a persistent *fortissimo* is likely to discourage the singers, causing them to give up the attempt. Some organists apparently think that the office of the organ is to drown the congregation! Ideally, the voices of the congregation should overflow the supporting tone of the organ.

The tempo of a tune should be carefully maintained throughout the singing of the hymn. There is often a tendency to slacken the pace after the first stanza. This may be due to difficulty in matching words and music and fatigue on the part of the singers or to the organist's broadening out the stanza endings. The habit of making a distinct retard at the end of each stanza is undesirable; it tends to make successive stanzas slower and slower. In the final stanza, however, a slight broadening out at the end is effective, but this should not be overmuch. Caution has constantly to be exerted in these matters. In some cases, the tempo should be carried up triumphantly to the Amen.

The organist should "play the hymn," and not merely play the tune over four, five, or ten times. Though the tune by virtue of its character gives atmospheric mood, it is the words which are of primary importance in congregational music. The tune merely gives added expression and warmth to the thought and emotion of the words. Now if the organist is to "play the hymn," he must know the words which the congregation are singing. In order that this may be so, the list of hymns and tunes for the service should be in his hands in time for him to familiarize himself thoroughly with them and consider various problems which may arise regarding their use. Either the hymn should be so well known by the organist that he is able to carry it in mind as he plays, or the tune should be sufficiently familiar for him to follow the words. Carrying along the thought of the hymn, the organist will impart, perhaps more or less unconsciously and subtly, meaning and vitality to its singing. He will give intelligent phrasing to the words and heightened expression to the thoughts they convey. This will take congregational music out of the class of the conventional and perfunctory and make it inspiring and valuable.

Musical expression in congregational music should be broad and general, not detailed. The dominant thought and feeling of a hymn should determine the general character of the tempo and registration. All stanzas need not, however, be played in precisely the same way. Quite the contrary. Though the registration and playing of a hymn should not "illustrate the words," there should be due regard for their changing general character. For instance, in the hymn "O God, the Rock of Ages," sung to the tune *Aurelia,* the second stanza, "Our years are like the shadows on sunny hills that lie," may best be played on manuals alone. The omission of the pedals in this stanza and their re-entrance in the following stanza, "O Thou, who canst not slumber," is expressive and effective. Varied expression may also be given different stanzas through slight variation of tempo and change of registration. In hymns like "O God, our help in ages past" and "In the cross of Christ I glory," in which the initial stanza recurs and becomes the final stanza, the last stanza may be sung in a deliberately broader manner than the first. Care, however, should be taken that contrasts in tempo are not excessive and changes in registration artificial. With large and resourceful organs expressive changes of tone may be made in different stanzas. Although the organs in many churches do not admit of much variety in congregational accompaniment, in more instances than one would ordinarily imagine at least some significantly expressive variation can be made. In the case of a long hymn, for instance, one of the middle stanzas might be played without pedals. But in no case should there be continual change of registration; a congregation should not be kept wondering what is going to happen next. Great and sudden changes, especially from loud to soft, should never be indulged in by the organist.

In seeking to make hymn singing an intelligent and effective exercise, the problem of adjusting the difference between verbal inflectional accents and musical accents frequently arises. Though the lines of a hymn in successive stanzas may have eight syllables and those of the tune eight notes, these may not uniformly coincide, for inflectional speech rhythms are varied, whereas musical rhythms are regular. For instance, in Bishop Ken's *Evening Hymn*, the first stanza begins "Glory to Thee," the second stanza "Forgive me, Lord." The verbal accent on "Glory" is on the first syllable, that of "Forgive" on the second. As the same tune is to be used for all stanzas, the musical and the verbal accents do not always agree. This disagreement may, however, be largely overcome if the organist "plays the words," feeling the word accent and not over-stressing the musical accent. Indeed, there should be a certain degree of flexibility within the rhythmic structure. Hymn singing should have a flowing character. This is one of its greatest glories. Now if the tune flows along with the words, as it can and should be made to do by phrasing it according to the words, the sense of the words may be preserved and at the same time a right musical feeling be maintained. By correct mental grouping of words and stressing of syllables, the verbal accents may readily and expressively override the otherwise rigid musical accents without in any way twisting the tune out of shape; the tune may to a degree conform to the words.

To secure life and vigor, phrase-ends should be duly regarded by the organist. An endless *legato* is deadening. The hands should be taken away from the keys at the ends of phrases, the organ, so to speak, breathing with the voices, but without the playing becoming choppy or losing that breadth which should characterize congregational music. A bit of silence at the end of lines will brace up indolent singers. Time for breathing should be taken from the last note of the phrase so that the following phrase may begin on time. This, however, is a matter which admits many exceptions. Tunes which are cast in the strongly metrical and rhythmic manner of the Victorian period are to be played and sung in stricter time than chorales and tunes of the earlier type, which are broad and free in style. But whatever the type of tune, there should not be indecision on the one hand, or angular regularity on the other. Between stanzas there should be a comfortable pause, one not too long or too brief. In some instances the employment of somewhat *staccato* style on the manuals against a *legato* pedal, especially if the pedal has a diatonically moving part, may animate the singing, giving it breadth and dignity. Where rhythmic stress or impetus is desired in congregational accompaniment, fewer notes should be tied over. If the organist is steady and discreet, and not freaky, the congregation will come more and more to have real confidence and repose in his leadership and enter more freely and fully into the spirit of the service.

An Amen should be in accord with the character of the hymn. The drooping, fade-away Amen, suggestive of timid abjection and mournful resignation, should be discarded. The Amen should be closely associated with the hymn of which it is the completion by general similarity and relatedness of tempo and volume of tone. A hymn sung *forte* should have a relatively *forte* Amen; one sung *piano,* a *piano* Amen. In a *forte* Amen there may be a slightly but not conspicuously diminished volume of organ support, so that vocal tone will be felt to be the characteristic element in congregational music. If this is done, the choir should be trained, and through them the congregation become accustomed, to sustain nearly the same general volume of tone in the Amen as in the hymn, even though the organ is not quite so large under the voices. It is well to make a clean cut between the hymn and the Amen, taking the hands off the keyboard, instead of stringing the last melody note of the tune over to the Amen. As the Amen is a ceremonial rather more than a conceptual item, it may properly be so treated that the hymn at its termination may have, so to speak, a beveled rather than a straight edge. The non-use of the pedals will often accomplish this.

The FUNCTION of the organ in choir music is naturally different from that in congregational music. As a musical body the choir is greatly superior to the congregation; it is more self-reliant and does not need the support and guidance which congregational singing demands. As a consequence the employment of the organ in choir music can be much more varied and artistically refined than would be possible in congregational music.

Choir music is essentially vocal music; the voices are central, the organ secondary. For the most part, the organ is an accompanying instrument, sustaining and animating the vocal parts. At times it may indeed surround the voices, but it should never eclipse them. Very frequently the organ dominates; we hear organ and voices rather than voices and organ.

Some choirs need more support and guidance than others. There is, however, a tendency for instrumental accompaniments to be overloud. Not only organists but orchestras often crowd the voices inordinately. This mistake in choir accompaniment is due to several causes. In the first place, organists do not sufficiently bear in mind that the range in volume of tone in an instrument like an organ is generally much greater than it is in choral bodies. Neither do they sufficiently realize that in the upper range of the organ loud stops are likely to be too strong in relation to the voices and thereby detract from the ensemble. In the second place, organists, feeling that the singers cannot stand securely on their own feet, give them too much support. Strong support may indeed be necessary in some instances, though how much is really needed is often a problem. The general tendency, however, is to use too much backing. Singers in many choirs are only too glad to lean on the all-enfolding tone of the organ. Then too, a loud organ may be used to cover up a multitude of sins—but two wrongs do not make a right!

An organ accompaniment which proves to be overloud is often caused by an indiscreet selection of music and by inadequate preparation. Half-learned music and music ill-adapted to the vocal capabilities of the singers may require the organist to use a big volume of tone to hold the choir together and avert disaster. An overbearing organ accompaniment is also frequently occasioned by the organist's carrying over into the service his use in rehearsal of an instrument to confirm notes and to incite expression. Choir expression in the service should be done by the voices and not by an over-reachingly prodding organ. Ideally, the organist ought to be free to devote his attention in the service to adjusting his part to the voices so that the ensemble may be made as perfect as possible.

To gauge his instrument aright an organist should know the relation of his organ tone to the vocal tone of the choir as heard in the church. This he may not be able to learn unless, through the kindness of some friend, he is able to hear it from the body of the church. Churches differ acoustically. Some organs are very deceptive, their location and the position of the keyboard being such that the organist does not accurately judge his own doings. The tone may go over the heads of both organist and singers, in which case the congregation find that the accompaniment is excessively loud while the organist and singers are wholly unaware of its being so.

The effectiveness of an anthem depends in large measure upon the nature of the accompaniment the organist supplies. The accompaniment should in fact be an integral part of the anthem and not something separate—an adjunct, a prop or a prod. It is part and parcel of the composition as much as the voices and should be so related and blended with them that there will be a unified and perfect ensemble, expressive and inspiring.

In MOST ANTHEMS the organ accompaniment duplicates the voice parts, supporting and in a measure coloring them. In such anthems the accompaniment should be neither feeble nor aggressive; with a feeble accompaniment the choir sounds flimsily supported, while an aggressive accompaniment makes it seem weak and struggling. The quality of tone the organist uses is important as well as the quantity. Generally it is desirable to use for the most part eight-foot stops, round and full, nicely supporting and blending with the vocal tone of the choir; sometimes, however, it is well to have the organ as a separate entity, distinctly a background, as when a comparatively full swell organ accompanies a unison choral passage. In accompaniments which duplicate the voice parts the organist too often uses—and uses continually—a sixteen-foot bourdon pedal. This is likely, especially in quieter passages, to give a sense of heaviness; one is very conscious of the organ accompaniment, for there is no double bass in the vocal score which is duplicated.

In anthems of elaborate character the organ often has an independent part. This may be either an embellishing melodic obligato added above the voices, or organ phrases alternating with choral phrases. In the case of the organ's having an embellishing or separate melodic part the adjustment of instrument and voices must be carefully considered, for passages which look very interesting on paper may lack clearness and distinctiveness in performance. When there are alternating instrumental and vocal balanced phrases, the choral parts must be firm and self-reliant and the organ be well-proportioned to the voices. Anthems with elaborate organ parts should not be undertaken unless there is an adequate instrument and a competent chorus.

Variety and impressiveness in choir music may be obtained by a temporary cessation of the organ—allowing the choir, at least once in a while, to sing some section of an anthem unaccompanied. This is too seldom done. In many instances it might be unwise to expose the choir to such a test; the thought of the possibility of singing unaccompanied sections or passages might, however, encourage the director to devote greater effort to beautifying and stabilizing the tone of his choir. An unaccompanied section now and then, not too long or complex in structure, may add greatly to the interest of the singers in their work as well as to the effectiveness of the anthem. As the accompaniment of most anthems is written in large notes throughout, the designation of an occasional passage for unaccompanied singing will necessarily be made by the organist or director.

In chanting it is not necessary for the organ continually to duplicate the voice parts—which the singers should practically know by heart. Changes in volume of tone in the accompaniment and also in tone color may give added expressiveness to the chanting. Moreover, some verses in the course of the Psalm may be sung by the voices in unison, with the chant melody sometimes freely harmonized on the organ. But such harmonization should be excellent, either improvised or composed by one competent in this line, and not a bizarre, freaky affair, the doing of a tyro. In unison verses, which are naturally majestic in character, the organ should, in most instances, be stronger than in the four-voiced accompanied verses, in order to balance the united voices of the choir. In quiet verses there may be considerable refinement of expression. For example, in the *Venite* the first half verse, "O worship the

Lord in the beauty of holiness" may be sung in unison by the upper voices alone, accompanied by light eight- and four-foot stops, the harmonized accompaniment being kept in the register above middle C, and the counter half verse, "Let the whole earth stand in awe of him" may be sung by the men's voices in unison with appropriate accompaniment on the organ in the lower vocal register. The treble portion might have an accompaniment of a clear flute-like quality, while the half verse sung by men's voices might have an accompaniment of a string or possibly diapason tone, solemn and august. Variations in the accompaniment of chanted parts in a service should, however, be sparingly used. They should never be sentimental, theatrical, displayful, or merely clever.

ORGANISTS as a rule spend too little time in serious study of the accompaniment of anthems. The conscientious organist plans his registrations ahead and leaves nothing to chance. The numerous pistons and other facilities which the modern organist has at his disposal tend to make him careless in the matter. His registration becomes stereotyped. Then too, in many churches one hears the vox celeste incessantly, while diapason, flute and dulciana are neglected. And in accompanying the choir in quiet passages how seldom are manuals employed without a clumsy sixteen-foot bourdon! It is wise for an organist every now and then to check up and see whether his accompaniments are not becoming dull and conventional through over-use of certain stops or combinations. If he finds he is at fault here, he should for a time forbid himself the use of this or that stop or combination and get out of the rut. By so doing he will often discover new excellencies in his organ. Organists often find fault with organs the possibilities of which they have not fully explored.

Not infrequently it happens that the registration of organists both in organ music and in choir accompaniment is not effective and telling because changes in the quality and volume of tone are not sufficiently distinct, so that the listener is conscious of any difference or contrast. The addition and subtraction of stops should be of significance. Unsignificant stop-changing is labor in vain. So also is the restless use of the swell-pedal. Convulsive "swell-pumping" is one of the organist's chief distempers. The swell-pedal should be used purposefully — for *crescendos*, for effecting phrasing and for contrasting the swell organ with boxes shut and boxes open. The normal position of the swell-box is closed. The greatest change effected by the swell-pedal is in the early stages of the opening of the shutters. Except in brilliant and stirring passages, it is often better, other things being considered, to accompany the choir with the swell-box closed than with it open. Then the tone has not so much edge; it is more remote, more mystical and more quietly sustaining—it is more churchly.

In the accompaniment of choir music the sense of bigness and breadth is often called for, but the full organ is too strong; a lesser volume of tone is suited to the choir—yet the sense of a full organ is needed. In many instances this may be obtained by building up a full organ in miniature, using the full swell amplified by two- or three-part chords in the middle register of a few foundation stops on the great organ, a fairly heavy pedal, and possibly swell octave couplers. But on different organs these ingredients will not be precisely the same.

Again, when the swell organ is used in accompanying a chorus in *mezzo forte* or *forte* passages and there is a single note common to several successive chords, an effective bit of registration may be had by holding this note in the middle register of the great organ on a full-toned stop of a gross flute or diapason quality, securing thereby a sustaining effect similar to that of the French horn in the orchestra.

ALTHOUGH ORGANS are much larger and more elaborate than formerly, many are not adapted for effectively accompanying the choir. The ordinary diapason on the great organ, planned for use in congregational singing and to serve as the basis of the full organ in the performance of organ music, is sometimes too big for choir accompaniment, unless the choir is a very large one. It sounds fat and bulky, and the vocal tone of the choir does not blend with it. Organ and voices seem to be on two different planes; the choir is dwarfed. A large-scaled but not over-loud open diapason is desirable for accompanying the choir in broad massive choral passages. The addition of such a stop would assure nobleness and stability and make it possible for loud passages in choir music to be dominantly vocal.

Another stop which would be of great value is a soft pedal bourdon for use in connection with organ music employing the lighter stops of the swell organ and in accompanying the choir in quiet passages. The usual bourdon pedal is too heavy; it gives the impression of insistence and clumsiness. A light pedal bourdon would blend with the vocal bass and would give impressiveness to quiet organ music. Such a pedal stop could be obtained by borrowing the sixteen-foot bourdon from the swell organ.

THE ORGANIST not only contributes impressive organ music but also gives virility and significance to congregational and choir music; and moreover, through his management of its various items, he gives continuity and elevation to the entire service. It is as a service-player rather than as a performer of solo organ music that he is distinctly a church organist. He is creator of a devotional atmosphere and interpreter of the choral and congregational parts with which he has to do. It is as a service-player that the church organist reaches the apex of his art.

The contribution of the organist to the service may be much or it may be little. The organist speaks through the organ. His religious perception is inevitably apparent throughout the service; much of its effectiveness depends upon him. The more perfect his work, the less obtrusive will it be—true art conceals art. Consciousness of high and significant contribution to the service and to the church is his highest reward.

CHAPTER XV

CONCLUSIONS AND SUGGESTIONS

To CONCEIVE and consider church music aright, we must look above its conventional practice; we must perceive the supreme realities and experiences of religion, together with the depth of expression which music is capable of giving these. The religious moods with which music has to do are profound and diverse: awe, exaltation and adoration, compassion and tenderness, resolve, courage, confidence and trust. To these various moods, church music gives beautifying and animating expression. It should, indeed, enlarge and stabilize their spiritual character in our consciousness, for, like words, music is a powerful and exalted means of religious expression.

Church music is clearly a dual subject—musical and religious. It is more than a musical matter; in true church music a religious element is present. This, as has been pointed out, is to be found in the conceptual factor, together with the ceremonial and associational factors, as these have been defined. Without a religious element, the music of the church is merely "music in church." How religious quality may be secured is one of the fundamental problems of church music. Many of the ways in which it may be attained have been noted in the preceding chapters. Others which either found no suitable place or were only hinted at should be considered here. First, is the use of the Christian year.

A more extensive and developed use of the Christian year in the services of Protestant churches would be very advantageous to their worship and to their use of choir music. At one time ultra-Protestants made no observance whatsoever of even the greatest of Christian festivals, Christmas and Easter. Just as they threw over liturgy with ritual, not perceiving that they

CONCLUSIONS AND SUGGESTIONS

were not identical, so in the case of the Christian year, finding in it what seemed to them abuse, they failed to recognize any useful feature in it. Curiously enough, there has been in recent times a revival both of the use of liturgy and of the observance of the Christian year; but in both cases there has been failure to secure their most salutary value. In the case of liturgy, there has been often a tinsel or an exotic "enrichment" of the service, and in the observance of the Christian year a flamboyant celebration of the isolated festival days of Christmas and Easter rather than an observance of the Christmas and Easter seasons. A larger regard for these seasons, and also an observance of other seasons, such as Advent and Whitsuntide, would not only give added interest and effectiveness to the services of the church, but would also aid the choir director very much in his planning and preparation.

The worship of the church and also church music could furthermore be improved by a better use of the church calendar. Aside from the fact that commonly in a four-page calendar one entire page is given up—possibly to save the cost of typesetting—to a repeated listing of all the church office-bearers, it should be noted that much of the data given regarding the musical parts of the service is of little value in furthering the religious effectiveness of the service. Who cares, and generally what difference does it make, who wrote the *Andante* played as the prelude, the *Cantabile* as the offertory, or the noisy *Finale* as the postlude? Then too, how slight is the value of knowing the first four or five words of a choir selection unless we are familiar with the rest? Instead of being constituted of routine and unsignificant material, the church calendar ought to be made a means of promoting worship. The printing of the texts of anthems used in the service, especially those which are not familiar, would be helpful. By presenting to the congregation texts which in themselves should have a message and are to be interpreted and illuminated by the music, the calendar would be a means of making the worship of the church more vital; it would, furthermore, eliminate straining to make

217

out the words being sung by the choir. And besides relieving the choir of undue exactions in the matter of enunciation in the more complicated music, it would serve the desirable purpose of exposing weak, inane, and unworthy texts which all too frequently are to be found in the choral portions of the service; thereby it would induce improvement.

As has been pointed out, the placement of the organ and choir affects church music. In recent years this matter has, fortunately, been given more consideration than formerly. The conception of the church building as an auditorium has yielded to that of the church as a place of worship. The platform arrangement with a pulpit in the centre and pulpit chairs behind has given way to the chancel arrangement with the communion table or altar as the centre and the reading desk and pulpit on the sides at the front. And musical arrangements have been changed to agree with the ministerial. The organ, formerly "high and lifted up" behind the minister, is now placed inconspicuously at the side, while the choir, formerly ranged behind the minister where the movements of its members, unnecessary and necessary, were often more or less disconcerting to the congregation, is now placed in the chancel, the most intimately consecrated part of the building, where it is usually divided, each half facing the other. No longer does the choir appear as a body on dress parade, singing to the people. The chancel location of the choir minimizes the tendency to regard the music of the church merely as "music in church" and the church musicians as performers. All this is to the good.

From the foregoing it will be seen that architects in building and remodeling churches may be agents in helping in the attainment of genuine church music. The interior arrangements of churches may be such as to create a right attitude on the part of the congregation toward church music and church musicians. Due consideration has not always been given to the location of the organ. Not a few churches have apparently been planned without thought that an organ was to be placed in them, the organ often appearing as a cumbersome piece of furniture, or if it is not awkwardly placed in the church, it is likely to be crammed into a small chamber in a side wall, more often than not a chamber having concrete sides and affording no proper breathing space for the instrument. Many organs are, in fact, buried at birth. It is not generally realized that ample height is especially desirable in an organ chamber. Moreover, care should be taken to relate the organ to the choir, placing it so as to give the choir a maximum of support with a minimum of instrumental covering.

It should not be overlooked that ushers, also, affect the worship and music of the church. Their office appears to have three aspects: welcoming people, inducing attendance on the part of those appointed to this duty, and making more dignified and reverential the assembling of the congregation. All three may not inappropriately be combined, but it is the last, that of aiding the congregation in assembling and preparing for the service, which is the most important. Ushers properly serve, so to speak, as acolytes for the congregation. All too often they are quite unaware of their very considerable influence on the devotional attitude and mood of the congregation at the beginning of the service, and through this on the effectiveness of the preliminary music of the service. People come to church with the intent and thought of worship. This attitude should be respected and this feeling deepened and not dispelled.

Sextons, also, it may be conjointly with architects, have influence on church music. Many churches are planned with inadequate ventilating facilities; and even those provided by the architect are not always sufficiently availed of by the sexton. Often churches have a stuffy atmosphere; the air is dead and stupefying. This has a dulling effect on the congregation and church musicians, and indeed on the music itself. By having the air in the church clear and fresh each Sunday, the sexton may render important service "Pro Gloria Dei."

It is not generally realized how many things which in themselves are small and commonly regarded as inconsequential enter into church music and affect its full attainment. Church music does not subsist in a vacuum, but in a world of human experience, physical and emotional.

THERE ARE FOUR major influences in the practice of church music: tradition and custom; the congregation; the clergy; and church musicians.

Current conceptions of church music and procedures in its practice rest in large measure upon tradition and custom. Tradition is not without significance, but it is likely to include at least a modicum of that which has become stereotyped, dry and sterile; and custom, which is not so deeply rooted as tradition and has often been developed rather casually without sound reason or adequate propriety, does not have the virility it ought to have. Tradition and custom undoubtedly possess features which are substantial and good, for the nature and character of religious worship cannot fail to induce much propriety in that which has constant association with it, but they are not to be depended upon entirely. Indeed, they may stand in the way of efficiency, hampering the efforts of clergy and church musicians and rendering the congregation dull and implastic. Tradition and custom should be scrutinized and be intelligently and effectively developed so as to become substantial and efficient aids to worship.

Secondly, the congregation has much influence on church music. It is capable, far more than their members generally realize, of making important contributions to the service and the effectiveness of church music in it. Their attitude and conduct not only affect the value of the service for themselves, but also react upon those charged with leading the services. Unfortunately, the true purpose of church music is not duly perceived and its design is often overlooked by a large proportion of those composing the congregation. Though the congregation, being a collective body, is usually quite inert, it nevertheless in one way and another largely affects church music. Against its predilections and inertia clergy and church musicians have often to contend.

CONCLUSIONS AND SUGGESTIONS

In congregationally governed churches, as has been noted, the influence of the congregation is much greater than in those which are clerically governed. In the Episcopal church, for instance, the music is officially in the hands of the rector, who may or may not call to his assistance one or more of the members of the parish, whereas in most other Protestant churches the control of church music is in the hands of the congregation or their representative, the music committee. The committee may indeed give consideration to the wishes and ideas of the minister, but they are free to act as they deem best. As the music committee is an administrative body, it is more important that its members be persons of discernment, discretion and fairness than that they themselves possess musical competence. Some committees are quietly efficient, while others are overbearing and blundering. Many of the troubles in choirs and much of the ineffectiveness of church music are occasioned by the music committee. Too often they conceive church music as a species of entertainment and treat it accordingly. Judging from the actions of many music committees one would infer that their chief and only duty was to exercise the lordly power of making appointments and discharges. That they have an obligation to support and aid their appointees is too seldom realized. Fortunately, however, there are committees who are admirable and stimulating, as many directors can testify. Such committees do high service to the church and to church music.

The minister is the third major influence in church music. Since he determines the substance and arrangement of the service and conducts it, it is largely in his power to bring it about that the musical portions of the service become vital, integral parts of it—that the music of the church becomes genuine church music.

Worship, being reflective and purposive in character, must have a certain continuity of mood. In securing this, music is of value. But on the other hand, the musical parts of the service are themselves in large measure dependent for their effectiveness upon what may be called their emotional context.

221

Properly, the musical parts should grow out of the service. For this to be so, they must be congruously related to those points of the service with which they are directly associated. Special care ought to be given to this matter, for mood does not shift rapidly, as for instance thought may in the sermon. Religious mood is almost always induced by an anterior purposiveness and intent; it does not burst spontaneously into being; moreover, it has, so to speak, an emotional overhang. As the minister has a comparatively free hand in molding the service, he may readily create a congenial and significant devotional environment for the musical parts, such as will enable them to render their full contribution to the service.

The spacing of the clerical parts of the service should be expressive. For instance, in the transition from Scripture reading to prayer, an impressive and natural pause, an interval in which there is, on the one hand, a sense of resting on Holy Writ and on the other that of rising to Divine Address, may lead profoundly into prayer. Such pauses are much like phrasing and inflection in expressive reading, but on a larger scale; they should be natural and inherent, and not mechanical and artificial. The devotional tone and temper of the clerical parts of the service affect the attainment of its musical parts to a greater extent than is ordinarily thought.

THE CHURCH MUSICIAN—the fourth major influence in church music—is generally regarded as being the sole influence. Unquestionably, as the active agent, he does have a position of great influence. But though the active agent, he is not a free agent; his doings are largely conditioned by tradition, by the congregation and clergy, as well as by the musical facilities and resources of the particular church.

Selected because of their musical competency, organists and choir directors naturally have a much more specific acquaintance with the musical features of their office than with its distinctly religious features. As most church musicians receive their training in the field of secular music, they are likely to be strongly imbued with the secular rather than with the religious spirit of performance. Moreover, like all artists, they are subject to the subtle temptation to become more absorbed in the manner and substance of their art than in its purpose. In their education slight attention is given to the distinctly religious side of church music. Whatever efficiency they may attain in the religious phases of their work is generally gained from tradition through the exercise of their office. Many of those having to do with church music were originally attracted to it by its musical appeal, and sometimes they remain chiefly interested in the musical side. The musical side should indeed be cultivated, but not at the expense of the religious; it should be developed in such a way as to enhance the religious effectiveness of church music.

Church musicians are generally enthusiastic workers, not infrequently maintaining their zeal under conditions which to others would be disheartening. Few laymen realize how devoted they are in their work. Unfortunately, their efforts are often ineffective because in one way or another they are not directed as intelligently and wisely as they should be. Conditions differ so much in different churches that church musicians are inevitably more or less individual workers; each must work out his own problems, relying on the exercise of common sense and such perception and discretion as he may possess. But though each director has in large measure to work out his own salvation, there are many matters in which he might be materially helped, his work lightened and made more successful. The church should see to it that church musicians are not left as struggling, isolated workers, often only tolerably effective. Higher ideals might be inculcated, appropriate materials and effective procedures suggested, and practical methods of musical attainment be presented.

In his efforts to attain genuine church music the church musician is in certain ways at a great disadvantage. Some things are beyond his ken, while others which affect it are not within his control. Naturally he is not deeply versed in liturgical material, nor is he an expert in service construction—he is a musician and not a liturgist. Many anthems which are musically good have texts which are devotionally superficial or obsolete. With current conceptions of church music as confused as they are, it comes about that the director in the selection of material and in its performance has an eye to securing a satisfactory musical make-up of the service rather than its devotional effectiveness. Then too, in the service the conditions for the realization of genuine music are often adverse. In many instances, there is no proper devotional attitude on the part of the assembling congregation, and choir numbers are placed in the service largely with the view of their giving variety. Having little or no devotional background or religiously expressive significance, the musical parts of the service tend to be regarded objectively, as "music in church." Against these and similar handicaps the church musician has to contend; they stand in his way of achieving his ideal. Sometimes, however, having become inured to that which is inferior and mediocre, he may not feel this as keenly as he ought.

Thus it is seen that there are four major influences in the practice of church music—tradition, congregation, clergy, and church musicians, and that none of them is as efficient and competent as it might and should be in its respective area. Furthermore, these influences often react detrimentally upon each other, with the result that there is a vicious circle of ineffectiveness. The church musician responds to the demands of the congregation, which are often unintelligent and blundering, and the minister likewise responds to their desires; church musicians feel themselves restricted and ministers are downcast over the situation. Then again, the church musician and the minister do not always see eye to eye in what should be a common task; each emphasizes aspects which are of particular importance to himself, to the neglect of others of equal or greater importance. The practice of church music is often a case of the blind leading the blind.

CONCLUSIONS AND SUGGESTIONS

CHURCH MUSIC is too large and too involved a subject to be left entirely to the individual musical director or clergyman. Here and there are individuals who make attainment considerably above the average, but these achievements are only local and usually temporary, depending for their continuation upon favorable conditions and the tenure of office of the given person. But even in these instances, church music is seldom all that it might be. A basic improvement in ideal and practice would undoubtedly be of very great value in these exceptional instances, as well as in the majority of churches. In churches generally, there is not a fully adequate conception of the function of church music or in their practice a full realization of its possibilities. Instead, the music of the church is likely to be largely a convention, a pleasant and diverting interpolation in the service, something with which to fill up the time, an opportunity for exhibition, a superficial attraction, or an allurement.

All blame for the failure of church music to attain its full value as an aid in worship cannot be laid at the door of the church musician, the clergy, or the congregation—any one or all three. Though none of these is without shortcomings, a fundamental and chief cause of failure is the fault of the system and procedure current in the churches. There is need of a radical, thoroughgoing treatment of the entire problem.

But how may this be effected? Where and by whom? Obviously the individual church may not promisingly undertake it, for church music is so complex and involved a matter and the conditions of its practice are so various that the specific treatment of it in an individual case cannot be taken as a universal solution. There must be principles and procedures based upon clear insight into the essential function of church music and adapted to the varying conditions of its practice. It is through a clearer understanding of the purpose and function of church music and the creation of conditions favorable to their attainment that improvement is to be secured.

MUSIC IN WORSHIP

CHURCH MUSIC is a church problem. The proper place for its fundamental, constructive study is in the theological seminary. Here all the requisites, except the purely musical, are present —courses in the conduct of worship, in religious education, in hymnology and liturgics, in Biblical interpretation, in church history and in parish administration. Courses in these special subjects, which in one way and another enter into the problem of church music, are not to be found elsewhere.

The seminaries are the radiating centres of religious education affecting the character and conduct of services in which music is employed. To care for church music as they should, the seminaries would, of course, have to acquire the requisite musical facilities and appoint a professor or instructor; but such an addition would only be making provision of means for attaining a use of music which would result in a greater effectiveness of the church service. Such a department would eliminate the unprofitable expenditures now made in the hope of attaining effective church music. It would directly affect the churches whose ministers had received its benefits; and through them, in the establishment of better church music and more effective procedures, its value would be extended to the church at large.

A general comprehensive course in the seminary should include the study of public worship and liturgics historically and analytically and a survey of the history of church music with detailed consideration of the various typical schools. It should also include a study of hymnology, hymn tunes, anthems, services, and other choir music. Early in the course the function of music in services of religious worship should be made clear. Later, typical conditions of its practice should be set forth and consideration given to practical problems which are most likely to arise. Ways of creating interest and effectiveness in congregational music and of attaining the true function of choir music should be presented and obstacles to their attainment noted. Suggestions should be made as to the arrangement and conducting of services so that the attitude created towards the musical parts will be such as to enable them to promote worship.

CONCLUSIONS AND SUGGESTIONS

The minister's various opportunities for creating high ideals and inducing effective practice should be pointed out and counsel given to enable him to be tactful as well as intelligent in his treatment of church music.

To aid the students in gaining actual acquaintance with and appreciation of the best church music, a considerable body of illustrative musical material should be used in the course. This may be obtained by means of a chorus maintained for this purpose and by phonographic records. In certain ways the chorus is superior to records: it is more intimate, it is more in accord with actual practice, and it is to be used in services. Records, on the other hand, are valuable in presenting, as no chorus could, music of varied types representing the best in different church-music traditions, Gregorian, Lutheran, Anglican and Russian. To be effective for the purpose, the chorus should be a permanent body. Ordinarily there would not be at hand in the seminary voices readily capable of rendering the desired music; furthermore, the time needed for preparation would probably not be available for students who already may have crowded schedules. A student choir, moreover, would have the disadvantage of changing considerably each year. A permanent group—composed, possibly, of members of choirs in the vicinity —would come to have a larger and more adequately prepared body of church music. This might to a degree counterbalance the advantages of intimacy acquired through participation. Some students, however, might be included in this body. The expense of maintaining such a choir should be assumed by the seminary as a laboratory or library expense necessary for the fullest attainment of the purpose of the course.

Besides this general course, there should be opportunity for extended study in the various phases of church music. Those who have interest and aptitude in special areas should be afforded an opportunity to develop these, as for instance, in hymnology. In this field, there is need of creative work voicing present day religious conceptions and aspirations. The religious life and conceptions of today should find embodiment and

227

exaltation in a contemporaneously created hymnology. It is not disparaging of the value of our hymnic inheritance to say that church music is carrying too much obsolete theological baggage. By such a course, students who are specially interested and apt in hymnic writing might, in their seminary or later years, make valuable contribution to the devotional literature of the church.

The daily services in religious seminaries ought to be so constituted and conducted as to be a means of education in worship and in church music. A keen devotional sense and feeling for genuine church music, sensitiveness and discernment, are largely obtained through experience. Liturgics and church music are at once both art and science—most deeply art, using that word in its vital sense. In order that the daily seminary services may have their full value for the student in gaining power in conducting worship, they should be led by persons having special competence in this particular field. Though it may be desirable to have the various professors in the seminary preach in the chapel services, it is not well to disregard the fact that some of them, being primarily teachers and devoting most of their time to scholarship, may have little ability of a high order in conducting worship. The conduct of worship should be entrusted to persons who are especially competent and gifted in doing this, not only members of the faculty but also ministers from outside. Devotional exercises would not then be a matter of mere routine in the seminaries and in the churches which these students will later serve. In the conduct of daily chapel services the department of church music should have an active part.

Although the seminary is the proper seat for the fundamental, critical study of church music, there are other educational institutions, in which its study should have place. In the college, where music is now generally included in the curriculum, a course in church music is pertinent and desirable. Youth is responsive to sacred music as well as to secular. A substantial course in the history, theory and practice of church music, treating the subject in both its musical and religious aspects, involves intellectual discipline and would promote religious insight and induce fine musical perception and judgment. A half-year course in church music, given every year or every other year, could be made illuminatingly educative. It is unfortunate that many who in their later years become actively engaged in church music and exercise a large influence in it should not have had the opportunity in their college days of gaining an understanding and appreciation of what is really possible in this field. It is surprising how many college graduates are to be found as choir singers, directors and members of church music committees.

The conservatory is another institution which is capable of helping the church in its music. Most conservatories offer facilities for the education of church musicians. In the smaller ones there are usually courses in organ playing and in choral conducting, and in the larger ones special courses in service playing, choir directing and management, in the history of church music, in plain song, improvisation, hymnology and liturgics. These institutions render most valuable service in training organists and choirmasters.

But not all who wish to become organists and choir directors are able to pursue extended courses in conservatories or to gain insight from a course in church music in college, to say nothing of attending courses in a theological seminary. They have to content themselves with organ lessons from their local teachers, gaining specific efficiency in church music from tradition, local custom and their own experience. These should be assisted in every way that the church, as a whole or denomination by denomination, may be able to provide.

The seminary might arrange regional extension courses to be conducted by the professor of church music. At meetings once a week, the purpose and function of church music could be set forth and ways of attainment be presented. Such courses should be pre-eminently practical, offering technical means and interpretational suggestions. Phonograph records, such as will imbue directors, organists and other church musicians with a sense of the right character and spirit of church music, should be liberally used and a considerable body of church music, both congregational and choir, be rehearsed with critical attention to defects and ways of correcting them.

Summer schools held under the auspices of the seminary, college, or conservatory, or by individual teachers may be potent means in the education of church musicians. With their daily meetings of classes, they may perhaps offer opportunity for a more ample study of church music than extension courses ordinarily would. Owing to the special facilities of each, there would naturally be a wide difference as to the exact character and amount of their offerings. In some instances, technical courses in organ playing, both elementary and advanced, courses in service playing and improvisation, in choral training and in harmony and other branches of musical theory could be included in the curriculum. Such a comprehensive schedule, offering opportunity for individual as well as group instruction, would probably require the services of more than a single instructor. Summer schools, conducted with right conceptions of church music, are of very great value in training efficient choir directors and organists for the churches.

Courses in church music may also be held in connection with summer religious conferences or institutes. A church music section in these could provide valuable instruction for church musicians and afford choir directors an opportunity of conferring with competent advisors regarding their individual problems. Moreover, lay workers attending the conference could be given opportunity to sing in a chorus presenting examples of the best church music, an experience which would be helpful for the conference and also later for the churches to which these church workers return.

Not only should church musicians be offered opportunities in formal education; provision should also be made for their growth and maintenance. Though choirmasters are largely self-directing workers, many of their problems being local and

CONCLUSIONS AND SUGGESTIONS

individual, and each having to work out many things for himself in the long travail of parish experience, there are matters in which the experience and knowledge of others would be most valuable. A clearing-house, where choir directors, and also ministers, music committees and other church committees, could go for assistance in matters pertaining to their offices, would be a great boon. For the choir director it should assemble a comprehensive library, books on the history, theory and practice of church music, a collection of the best anthems, services, responses and chants, together with the most desirable organ music for church use. Such an institution would relieve churches of much unfruitful expense and choirmasters of unproductive effort in searching for desirable material.

Furthermore, such a clearing-house could furnish church committees entrusted with the erection or remodeling of churches sound information and unbiased advice as to architectural and financial problems they might encounter. It could be a place to which committees charged with the purchase of a new organ or the remodeling of an old one could resort for advice in dealing with matters in which they naturally have little knowledge or no experience. Valuable counsel could be secured as to specifications and details of organ construction and also as to the effective placement of the instrument.

DUE REGARD should ever be given to making church music not only effective but worthy. That "a thing works" is not the only criterion in life—or in church music. The quality and character of the music and the manner of its use are matters of consequence. Regard should be given them, for there is real danger of music's giving a false impression and actual misrepresentation of religion. The music used in the church service should not be either of a saccharine or a flamboyant character; neither should its employment be such as to appear trivial or unworthy. Sincerity of the highest order should characterize the worship and services of the church—and this, of course, includes both the character of the music and the manner of its use. Through

231

its power of expression and impression, church music should be a means of making religion attractive and meaningful in its true, exalting character.

Church music has many interrelated aspects and phases, some of which are far from simple. Yet without over-simplifying its problems or treating them superficially, it can be seen that there are certain ideals and principles which should essentially govern its practice. Some areas in its practice are subject to fundamental principles, while others are indeterminate and very variable and have to be treated as best they may through the discernment and the discretion of those in charge. There is no simple, universal formula. Nevertheless, typical conditions may be set forth and means of making them favorable for the attainment of genuine church music may be designated. Above all and guiding all, the great and high purpose of church music may be made clear and inspiring. There will, however, always be a call for living intelligence. Others may chart the seas and provide the compass, but each must sail his own ship.